ANCIENT CHURCHES

Ancient Churches of Sussex

Ken & Joyce Whiteman

Roedale Books

First published 1994

© K & J Whiteman 1994

All rights reserved. No part of this book may be
reproduced or transmitted in any form
without permission in writing from the Publisher.

British Library Cataloguing–in–Publication Data

A catalogue record for this book is available from the British Library.

ISBN 0 9522560 0 2

Published by
Roedale Books, 419B Ditchling Road, Brighton,
East Sussex BN1 6XB, England.

Printed and bound in Great Britain by
BIDDLES LTD.,
Guildford, Surrey.

Cover photograph : Southease
Title page : Playden

Contents

Introduction	7
The Churches	9
Bibliography	187
Glossary	188
Map	191

Introduction

Between August 1988 and September 1991 we walked to all the ancient churches of Sussex. Our main interest was in the buildings of medieval date but, since so few churches were built between the Reformation and 1800, we included these too. For the purposes of this book, therefore, an ancient church is one with its walls, completely or in part, built before 1800 and still visible today. There are 278 churches which come into this category and we visited them all. Several churches built *after* 1800 incorporate old furnishings and memorials, even medieval arcades, but these are not included.

Initially we made notes and took photographs for our own benefit, only later deciding to produce a gazetteer of the old parish churches of Sussex. Others have done this before. Frederick Harrison wrote his 'Notes on Sussex Churches' in 1906, just after the period of Victorian restorations. Pevsner and Nairn wrote about the churches in the Sussex volume of 'The Buildings of England' in 1965. Many changes have occurred since then. Churches have been deconsecrated and found other uses as shops, arts centres and museums. Interiors have been re-ordered and old furnishings displaced. Modern scholarship offers new insight into aspects of church history. We have aimed to give an up-to-date account.

We have only written about things we have seen, except for the bells which are rarely visible; for these we have relied mainly on Elphick's 'Sussex Bells and Belfries'. Our book offers only a brief introduction to each church. It is not a substitute for the many excellent guides which go into greater detail and are available at the churches.

No attempt is made to recommend churches. We found things of interest in all that we visited. There are, of course, some that are particularly appealing to us and, as has been very evident, every church is special to its parishioners.

We are frequently asked if we found many churches locked. Most were open to visitors during daylight hours; about one in ten were closed. Occasionally a card in the porch gave the name and address of a key-holder. More often there was a notice giving times when the church would be open for visitors, a facility often provided regularly in summer.

Walking in the countryside and studying old churches have been two of our enthusiasms for many years. For us, therefore, the pleasure and satisfaction gained from visiting the Sussex churches was enhanced by walking to them, often along paths trodden by parishioners for centuries. Sussex has a wealth of footpaths, bridleways and country lanes and, with the help of large scale Ordnance Survey maps (1:25000), it was not difficult to plan walks of 5–10 miles with two or more churches en route. By walking to them all we enjoyed the varied scenery of East and West Sussex: the Downs, the Weald, the coastal plain, the river valleys.

We want to thank the many parish clergy, church wardens and keyholders who helped us with such kindness and hospitality. We acknowledge the assistance given to us by the librarian and staff of the Sussex Archaeological Society Library at Barbican House, Lewes. Thanks are also due to the colleagues who helped greatly in the typesetting and production of this book.

K & J Whiteman, Brighton 1993

The Churches

Each entry begins with the parish or place where the church is situated, followed by the dedication, where known.

A two-figure map reference is given indicating the square of the National Grid in which the church is to be found. (See the map of Sussex on p191.)

Abbreviations used in the text are N,S,E and W for north, south, east, and west when used as adjectives and c. and d. for 'circa' and 'died' when followed by a date.

Albourne *St Bartholomew*

The church stands in quiet countryside away from the village; a path from the churchyard leads to the alder stream from which Albourne takes its name. Little remains of an earlier Norman church; the present building, of flint with stone dressings under a Horsham slab roof, is mainly the result of a restoration in 1859. The nave, N aisle and S porch are Victorian but the chancel dates from the 12th century. The chancel arch with chevron decoration is a copy of the original arch, most of which is built into the W wall of the churchyard. In the chancel (S) is a blocked Norman window. The imposts in the E wall are of similar age and may be the remains of an apse; the 13th-century pointed arch above is backed by a wall containing a lancet window. The trefoil-headed piscina is 13th-century. In the nave floor is a small inscribed brass dated 1603. The medieval font, a plain octagonal bowl and stem, stands on a large slab of Sussex marble.

Blocked Norman window

Alciston

Alciston was a Saxon settlement. By the time of the Domesday Survey it was a wealthy estate in the possession of Battle Abbey; the monastic tithe barn and the ruins of a 14th-century dovecote can be seen from the churchyard. The church consists of a large chancel, a long nave with a small weatherboarded bell turret and a N porch. Excavations in 1984 uncovered foundations of the apse of a pre-Conquest church. The main structure of the present church may well be Norman, indications being a round-headed chancel window and the thickness of the walls. In the 13th century the chancel was altered (note the lancet windows and blocked doorways) and the porch added. The chancel was shortened in the 15th century and the

Porch doorway

Perpendicular E window and a low side window inserted. In 1951 the porch was rebuilt but the Early English doorway with moulded arch and shafts was reset. On the exterior walls are several mass dials.

Aldingbourne *St Mary* 90W

A mainly Victorian exterior conceals the 12th-century origins of Aldingbourne church. St Mary's has a long nave and chancel with no division between, a S aisle, S porch and a N tower. Part of the Domesday church exists in the W and N walls of the nave. In the early 12th century a N aisle was built (later demolished) and the blocked Norman arches can still be seen in the nave, some with traces of original painting. The dominant feature inside is the five-bay Transitional arcade (late 12th-century) with its round pillars, scalloped capitals and pointed arches. Of similar date is the S doorway, now enclosed by a 17th-century porch. The 13th century saw the building of the chancel, the lower stages of the tower and the stone vaulted chapel in the aisle. Dogtooth ornament is used on the vaulting ribs and the sedilia in the chancel. The W doorway, also Early English, has grotesque label stops. There are two fonts; one is 12th-century, a square bowl with shallow arcading, the other small and roughly shaped, possibly of greater age. Also of note are a consecration cross by the W door, remains of painted biblical texts and the Royal Arms of William III.

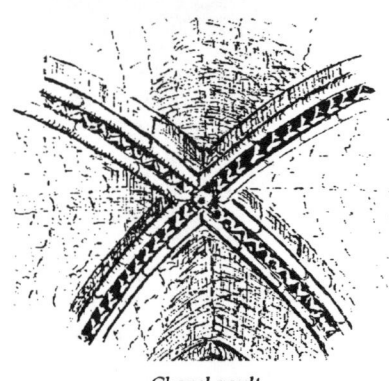
Chapel vault

Alfriston *St Andrew* 50

This imposing cruciform church, built entirely in the 14th century, has walls faced with coursed flints, skilfully knapped and squared. Rising above the central tower is a shingled broach spire. A spacious interior has an aisleless nave and a large crossing. Lofty arches are supported by pillars with concave sides and capitals. The window details are of architectural interest, demonstrating the transition from the flowing tracery of the Decorated style (N transept and chancel) to the panel tracery of the Perpendicular period. Old glass representing the figure of St Alphège can be seen in the upper lights of the N transept window. In the chancel S wall are the richly decorated sedilia and adjoining piscina, and on the N side is an Easter Sepulchre. A piscina in each of the transepts indicates their former use as chapels. Close by the church stands the clergy house, a timber-framed dwelling built about 1350 for parish priests. It was the first property bought by the National Trust.

Central tower

Amberley *St Michael*

Amberley castle, overlooking the Arun floodplain, belonged to the Bishops of Chichester until the 16th century; the church, alongside its walls, has gained from the patronage of its neighbour. The building of nave and chancel is believed to have been started by Bishop Luffa c.1100, the exterior N wall with round-headed windows and a blocked doorway indicating the church's Norman origins. In the 13th century, when the powerful bishop was also Chancellor of England, the W tower, a larger chancel and a S aisle were added. A huge tiled roof covers the high nave and aisle. The S porch encloses a doorway of c.1300. Inside, the nave is clearly Norman. Three round-headed windows under moulded arches have flanking shafts. There is zig-zag decoration on all three orders of the chancel arch which are supported by triple responds and shafts with scroll and foliage carving. The three-bay arcade and lancet windows of chancel and aisle (W and E) date from the 13th century. South of the chancel arch are remains of 12/13th-century wall paintings; there are two painted consecration crosses on the nave walls. The Norman font is square with shallow arcading. In the S aisle a brass of 1424 shows a man with sword in a surcoat decorated with lions' heads.

Chancel arch capital

Angmering *St Margaret* 00

Extensive building work was undertaken in 1853 by the architect S.S.Teulon and the present church is mainly the result of his reconstruction. Unaltered, however, is the late Perpendicular tower (1507) of flint and ashlar arranged in a chequered pattern. This was built by Syon Abbey whose arms, along with the date between two crosses, are carved on a stone above the W door. It has a NE stair turret, two-light bell-openings and a battlemented parapet. The internal arch to the nave is high and of three orders. From the earlier building survive the chancel arch (c.1200), the arch to the S chapel and the S door (re-sited). In the nave floor is a small brass to Eden Baker (d.1598) who is portrayed wearing a tall, broad-brimmed hat. The font, pulpit and the chancel fittings were designed by Teulon.

Brass effigy, 1598

Apuldram *St Mary the Virgin* 80W

There is no village; the church stands in fields south of Fishbourne. The chancel, nave and S aisle are 13th-century though remains of a 12th-century church, built as a chapel of ease to Bosham, exist in the nave N wall. The 15th-century S porch has an unusual mass dial on the E window sill using the jamb as a gnomon. There is no interior division between nave and chancel which are under a continuous roof; the three-bay nave arcade has circular pillars and chamfered arches. The chancel is a notable example of Early English church architecture. Triplets of lancet windows, larger and stepped in the E wall, have rich mouldings and Purbeck marble shafts; a string course runs below. Recessed in the S wall is a trefoil-headed piscina. A large 13th-century graveslab on the floor is carved with a floriated

Chancel windows

cross. Medieval features elsewhere are the rood loft stairs (nave N wall), a piscina with credence shelf (aisle S wall) and a squint with a trefoil opening (arcade E respond). A 15th-century oak screen has ogee arches with quatrefoils in the spandrels. The square Norman font has carved shallow arcading.

Ardingly *St Peter* 32

A few stones remain of an earlier 12th-century church at Ardingly and one, a Norman capital, is displayed in the N aisle. The present church, built of local sandstone, has a nave, chancel and S aisle dating from 1325-50; there are windows with Decorated tracery typical of the period. The low tower and timber-framed porch were added in the 15th century and the N aisle and vestry are Victorian. The nave S arcade of two wide bays has an octagonal pillar and responds with attached shafts. A doorway in the N wall gave access to a former rood loft. An ancient tower staircase to the first floor is constructed of baulks of timber cut diagonally. The finely carved chancel screen is early 15th-century and the communion rail of turned twisted balusters dates from c.1700. In two chancel windows, which have unusual wooden hoodmoulds, are medieval stained glass shields. Particularly notable are the brass memorials which are of high quality and well preserved. On the chancel floor are brasses of the Wakehurst and Culpeper families who lived at nearby Wakehurst Place. A tomb chest in the sanctuary carries a brass to Richard Wakehurst (d.1454) and his wife with figures under crocketed canopies.

Canopied brass

Arlington *St Pancras*   50

The church was described in the 19th century as being 'in a state of decay, dirt and ruin'. Subsequent restoration did not destroy its ancient features. The nave is Saxon; there is long and short work visible at three of the corners and above the porch is a double-splayed window with Roman bricks forming the head of the arch. North of the chancel is a Norman chapel with two narrow round-headed windows in the N wall and a small circular window in the W gable. The capitals of the interior W arch have deeply incised dogtooth ornament. The short tower is Early English and has a shingled broach spire set well below the ridge of the nave roof. In the 14th century the chancel, N aisle and arcade were rebuilt in the Decorated style. The chapel E window has reticulated tracery, the chancel a more unusual design of arches upon arches. There is a curious castellated piscina. The roofs have old moulded tie-beams with crown-posts and bracing. Several medieval graveslabs, tapered and with raised crosses, can be seen in the chancel and chapel. The square stone font dates from the Perpendicular period.

Saxon window

Arundel St Nicholas

Stone pulpit

Arundel church is a large cruciform structure in the early Perpendicular style. It was completely rebuilt c.1380 as a collegiate church with the eastern wing, the Fitzalan chapel, belonging to the college of canons. After the Reformation this part was sold to the Earl of Arundel and it remains today a private Roman Catholic chapel entered from the castle. The rest of the building is the parish church and consists of an aisled nave with transepts, a low tower and spire above the crossing, a stone S porch and an old wooden N porch. The exterior is faced with knapped and squared flints. Inside are five-bay arcades with compound pillars and hollow-chamfered arches. Perpendicular windows with panel tracery light the aisles; the clerestory windows are quatrefoils. Behind the altar is a huge screen of Sussex wrought iron through which are seen the monuments in the Fitzalan chapel. This unique piece of ironwork dates from the building of the church. Also 14th-century are the wall paintings in the N aisle (the Seven Acts of Mercy, the Seven Deadly Sins), the font of Sussex marble (octagonal, with panels of cinquefoil arches) and the stone pulpit, one of only two in Sussex of medieval date.

Ashburnham *St Peter* 61

Ashburnham Place was formerly the seat of the Earls of Ashburnham; beside it in the park is St Peter's. The oldest part of the church is the 15th-century 'Pelham' tower. The rest was rebuilt in 1665, mainly in the late Gothic style. The walls are battlemented and finials decorate the gables. Inside, the nave is a wide chamber lit by four large windows of intersecting tracery under four-centred arches. A flight of seven steps leads up to a chancel with N and S chapels, the latter with a gallery that was the private pew of the Ashburnhams. The N chapel contains two large marble monuments. A tomb chest has recumbent effigies of John Ashburnham (the builder of the church, d.1671) and his two wives; beneath are figures of his kneeling children. In contrasting, dramatic style is the memorial to William Ashburnham (d.1679) and his wife, she reclining on one arm, he kneeling nearby backed by canopy and draperies. Many of the

Chancel railings

original furnishings remain: a wooden W gallery on Ionic columns, oak pulpit, panelling and box pews (since made lower), the N door, the marble font and iron railings across the arches to tower, chancel and chapels. From later in the 17th century are the rare three-sided communion rail and the former reredos (now on the nave S wall), a painting in oils of Aaron, Moses and religious texts.

Ashington St Peter & St Paul

Bellcote

Ashington church originated in the 12th century as a chapel of ease in the parish of Washington; subsequently Ashington became a parish in its own right. In the last century its church was a small 15th-century structure with undivided nave and chancel, a S porch and a bell turret with a low shingled broach spire. In 1871 the church was altered to the form we see today; the nave was extended to the west, a S aisle of five bays added, the S porch rebuilt and an open bellcote raised at the W end. From the old church, Perpendicular windows were re-used in the W, N and E walls and a holy water stoup of the 14th or 15th century was reset by the S door. The church possesses a 14th-century bell. In the churchyard are carved gravestones of the 18th century.

Ashurst St James

Ashurst is a scattered community to the north of Steyning. Its small church has a 12th-century nave with a round-headed doorway in the N wall. A south aisle (wider than the nave) and arcade (round pillars, moulded capitals) were added c.1200. Slightly later is the N extension of the nave and the SW tower, supported by semi-circular responds and capitals with stiff-leaf decoration. The chancel with trefoil-headed lancets is 13th-century. Various materials are used on the roofs: Horsham slabs, tiles, shingles on the short broach spire. A single wide span of Horsham slabs covers the body of the church supported inside by a long beam stretching across nave and aisle. The 13th-century font has a square bowl incised with pointed arcading on one side. On display in the nave is a vamphorn, one of only eight in the country. This primitive musical instrument, made in 1770, was probably used to provide a droning accompaniment to the choir.

The Ashurst vamphorn

Balcombe *St Mary* ✓

The larger part of the present building, nave, chancel and N aisle, is Victorian; surviving from the ancient church are the SW tower and the former nave and chancel (now the S aisle and chapel). The 15th-century tower is made of sandstone blocks and has a shingled broach spire. The aisle and chapel have been so rebuilt that it is difficult to date them. Outside are numerous and varied post-Reformation churchyard memorials. Chest tombs of the 17th century and later (28 in all) stand close together. Gravestones of the 18th century are carved with trumpets and angels. There are several stone memorials of a type peculiar to Sussex; these consist of two short posts with polyhedral heads joined by a horizontal beam. They are modelled on wooden graveboards, cheap but impermanent memorials of the 17th century onwards.

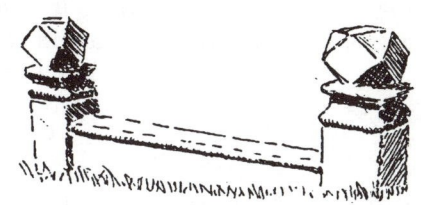

Churchyard memorial

Barcombe *St Mary the Virgin* ✓

Barcombe is a community of three parts. Barcombe Mills on the Ouse is the site of the mills mentioned in Domesday Book. Barcombe Cross is where the village was re-sited after a visitation of the plague in the 17th century. Barcombe itself is the site of the original village, now just a farm, a few houses and the church. The N wall of the nave dates from c.1100, the squat tower with shingled broach spire and the chancel from the 13th century. Inside, the S arcade is of two dates. The eastern opening has a simple chamfered arch with no capitals (13th-century) which once led into a transeptal chapel; the two western openings have octagonal pillars and decoration of c.1400. In the 19th century the present S aisle was built, the exterior of the church was refaced and

Broach spire

old memorial slabs set in the walls. The font (14th-century) has a square bowl carved with patterns of arches and crosses. A nave window contains 17th-century armorial stained glass. On the aisle wall is a huge memorial of 1730 in white marble with scrolled pediment supported by life-sized female figures. A recent gift to the church is the engraved glass screen filling the tower arch.

Barlavington St Mary   91W

The church, near a farm and a few houses, looks south to the wooded slope of the western Downs. It is built of local stone from both the Upper and Lower Greensand and consists of nave with S aisle, chancel and a W bellcote. The windows are mainly Early English lancets, the exception being the W window which has two lancets with a round light above. In the N wall is a blocked arcade. Within, the two-bay Transitional S arcade has a central round pillar with square abacus and pointed arches which indicate a date of c.1200. The lancet windows are set in splays with scoinson arches, dropped inner arches to reduce the height required for the splay; these are of a slightly later date. The S aisle, although of similar style to the rest of the church, was rebuilt in the 19th century. The E wall of the chancel has two lancets separated by a recess in which stands a modern carving of the Annunciation. Sussex has a wealth of simple Early English churches and St Mary's is a good example.

West window

Barnham St Mary   90W

A church at Barnham was recorded in the Domesday Survey. The thick flint walls of the nave are Norman as are the two small windows high in the S wall. In the late 12th century a N aisle was added, but exactly when this was demolished is uncertain; remains of the arcade are visible in the N wall. There is a white weatherboarded bell turret at the W end and a much restored 13th-century S porch. Inside, the one surviving bay of the arcade accommodates the organ and gives access to the modern vestry. A timber construction with arched braces divides the nave from the 13th-century chancel which has deeply splayed lancet windows with a moulded string course beneath. In the E wall is an elegant group of three lancets, the central one taller, filled with 20th-century stained glass. A trefoil-headed piscina in the S wall has roll moulding (the bowl is modern); a second piscina in the nave, also 13th-century, indicates the site of a former altar. The Norman font is a square bowl of Sussex marble with traces of decorative arcading. Interesting graffiti on a jamb of the N bay, protected by a glass panel, include crosses and a medieval inscription.

Bell turret

Battle *St Mary*   71E

Battle Abbey was built to commemorate the Battle of Hastings. A small town grew up at its gates and in 1115 Abbot Ralph founded a church nearby to serve the community. This first church was mainly rebuilt c.1200 and enlarged during the medieval period. Entrance is through the 15th-century battlemented tower. In the nave, five-bay Transitional arcades to aisles have alternate round and octagonal pillars with foliage capitals; above are clerestory lancet windows. Early 14th-century paintings on the N wall depict scenes from the life of St Margaret of Antioch. The square, arcaded font is Norman, its 15th-century painted cover the earliest of four medieval font covers in Sussex. There are fragments of 15th-century glass in the N aisle windows. The Early English chancel has three original windows (S). Beneath an arch is the richly carved alabaster tomb with recumbent figures of Sir Anthony Browne (d.1548) and his wife. The N chapel, enlarged in the 14th century, has a double piscina. In the 15th-

The Browne monument

century S chapel is a three-light window with Perpendicular tracery and a tall niche on each side. The church displays a 'Breeches Bible'. Memorials include brasses and a tablet to the inventor of the power loom, Edmund Cartwright. In the churchyard (E) is the grave of Isaac Ingall, an Abbey servant, who died aged 120.

Beckley *All Saints* 82E

The oldest part of the church is the lower stage of the W tower, built c.1100, which has herringbone work typical of the early Norman period. There have been many alterations to the original building. In the 13th century the S aisle was added. The 14th century saw the rebuilding of the chancel and the addition of the N aisle, chapel, S porch and the upper stage of the tower with its broach spire and turret stairway. Extensive restoration took place in the 19th century and the S chapel was added. Inside, the three-bay nave arcades have double-chamfered arches on octagonal pillars. The chancel E window with reticulated tracery dates from c.1320; in the S wall are sedilia and ogee-arched piscina. Two windows in the N chapel are of the 14th-century. Steps and a doorway high in the wall gave access to a former rood loft; below is a piscina under a pointed arch. The 18th-century font is a fluted bowl of white marble; preserved nearby is a fragment of an earlier Norman font. Other interesting details are the 'Green Man' carvings on corbels in the W and N walls, the tower screen with twisted balusters (formerly the 17th-century communion rail) and the dugout church chest with ancient ironwork and three locks.

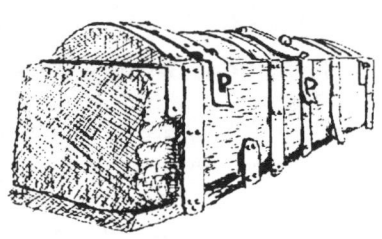
Dugout chest

Beddingham *St Andrew* 40

Beddingham, near Lewes, is a large agricultural parish; there is no village. Of the original Norman church only the nave walls and one blocked window (N) remain. The arcades (c.1200) are strong features. The S arcade has low square abaci on massive pillars and dates from the Transitional period; on the E arch is 13th-century painted decoration. In the S aisle is a window with plate tracery. The N arcade has round abaci and pointed arches with a slight chamfer. Clerestory windows were inserted during the Decorated period and at that time the aisles and chancel were rebuilt. There is a three-light Decorated E window; other chancel windows are elegant trefoil-headed lancets, one, in the S wall, a low side window. The large 16th-century tower is built in a basically chequered arrangement of stone and flints; it is battlemented and has a low pyramidal cap.

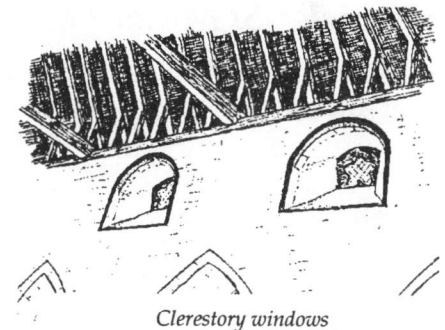
Clerestory windows

Bepton *St Mary* 81W

Bepton is one of several quiet hamlets on the narrow road below the Downs near Midhurst. Its early 13th-century church was greatly restored in 1878 but the W tower, nave S wall and doorway remain from the original building. The low tower is of two stages under a pyramidal roof; one lancet window in the N wall is 13th-century and there are square-headed belfry openings. Large diagonal buttresses are of brick and date from the 17th century. The interior arch to the nave, pointed and unchamfered, is 13th-century; the chancel arch is modern. The chancel has one 13th-century window (N wall). Set in the floor by the vestry door is an ancient tapering graveslab, over 2m long, carved with a four-circled cross. A tomb recess c.1300 is under a large pointed arch with crocketed sides and a decorative finial. The Lombardic inscription, rather damaged, has been translated as 'Rado de la Hedol lies here. God grant him the greatest mercy'.

Tomb recess

Berwick *St Michael & All Angels* 50

Berwick is one of a line of villages set on the narrow Greensand belt under the eastern end of the Downs. All their churches are old foundations and all are set on mounds that may be of even greater antiquity. Berwick church has a chancel, nave with aisles, N and S porches and a W tower with shingled broach spire. Most of the church and window details appear to date from the 13th to 15th centuries, although much is obscured by the 17th and 19th-century restorations. The oldest feature is the font which possibly survives from an earlier church and has the tower wall and pillar of the S arcade built around part of it. In the chancel N wall is a large canopied recess, used in medieval times as an Easter Sepulchre. The church is notable for its 20th-century paintings by Duncan Grant, Vanessa and Quentin Bell which cover the walls, screens and pulpit. These were commissioned by Bishop Bell of Chichester and painted during World War II.

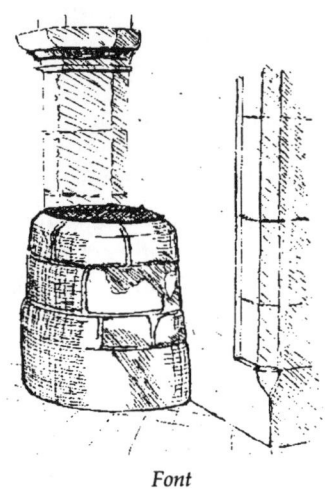
Font

Bexhill *St Peter* 70E

St Peter's is in the Old Town of Bexhill, a mile inland from the seaside resort. The present church owes as much to the restorations of 1868 and 1907 as to earlier times. The aisles, chancel and S porch are modern, the W tower, nave arcades and N chapel ancient. Externally the tower looks Perpendicular but from inside is seen to be Norman in its lower stages with round arches in the N and S walls to the aisles and a Transitional arch to the nave. The two western bays of the arcades, also Norman, have round arches on circular pillars and capitals showing a variety of 12th-century ornament; these arches are actually cut through the walls of an earlier, Saxon church. The third bay is a 13th-century extension and the remaining bays are the Victorian lengthening of the nave. To the north of these is a 15th-century chantry chapel with a fine traceried E window which now gives onto the organ chamber. In a N aisle window are pieces of medieval stained glass, an Annunciation and figures of Saints. On the tower walls are two stone memorials. One is a large tapering grave-slab of the 13th century carved with a floriated cross. The other is a coffin lid found beneath the nave floor in the 19th century, richly ornamented with Saxon interlace carving, one of the finest in the country.

Saxon coffin lid

Bignor *Holy Cross* 91W

Bignor comprises a rectangle of narrow lanes with adjoining houses, farms and a church. The church consists of chancel, aisled nave, S porch and W bell turret. The nave is wide and very high; the plain Norman chancel arch reaches only halfway up the E wall. Two-bay N and S arcades are Early English with round pillars and double-chamfered arches differing slightly in period and detail. On the south the inner order of the arch is supported at the responds by half-shafts, on the north by corbels; the S pillar has deeper moulding than the N, indicating greater age. In the chancel the windows are lancets (replacements), the E window consisting of three side-by-side with a small round opening above. The chancel screen, one of the earliest in Sussex, is of 14th-century date with similar decoration to the small screen at Rodmell. The simple Norman font is tub-shaped, roughly finished.

Chancel screen

Billingshurst *St Mary*

Roman Stane Street, now a busy main road, runs through the centre of Billingshurst; on higher ground above it is St Mary's church.

Churchyard and W tower

Dominating the western approach is the shingled broach spire, broad and tall, crowning the 13th-century W tower, one of the oldest parts of the church; an original lancet remains in the S wall. A large clasping buttress (S) contrasts with a smaller angle buttress (N); between them is a brick and timber Tudor porch leading to a W entrance. Inside, the aisled nave has N and S arcades with octagonal pillars and double-chamfered arches; the aisle windows date from the 15th century (S) and the 16th century (N). A fine wagon roof in the nave has square panels and, at the intersections, carved bosses of different designs now reproduced on tapestry kneelers. The chancel is modern but its S chapel is 13th-century with two lancets and a low priest's doorway. On the chancel N wall is a memorial to Edward Gorringe (d.1617) and his wife shown with their kneeling children. A late 15th-century brass in the nave floor has small effigies of Thomas Bartlet and his wife.

Binsted *St Mary*

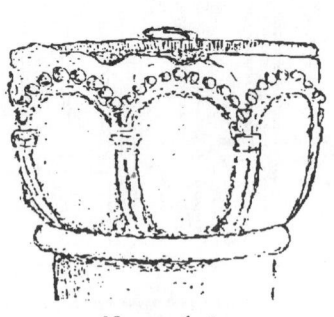
Norman font

Binsted, approximately two miles west of Arundel, consists of a farm, a few cottages and a small church with shingled bell turret. Of the original 12th-century building remain the walls and three round-headed windows; porch and vestry were built during the 19th-century restoration. The aisleless interior has no arch between nave and chancel which are divided by simple timber framing. In the splay of one window (N) is a 12th-century wall painting of St Margaret of Scotland on one side and on the other a triple branched tree, possibly symbolising the Tree of Life. The two stained glass panels in the E window were designed by Henry Holiday; the windows and pavement in the chancel were made by Powell in the 19th century. The piscina and triangular headed recess date from the 12th century. The Norman font is bowl-shaped and ornamented with carved arcading.

Birdham *St James* 80W

Birdham, on the shore of Chichester Harbour, was one of the places granted to (St) Wilfrid by Caedwalla in 683. The earliest part of the present church is the nave, its 14th-century date apparent from the chancel arch, a small trefoil-headed piscina in the S wall and the S doorway. The roof may also be of this age though most of the billet decoration is a later addition. There is evidence that the tower was built c.1545; it has a massive stair turret on the S wall and a pyramidal cap within battlements. The chancel and S porch were rebuilt in the 19th century; a large N vestry was added recently. On display in the church is a rare 14th-century tile found when the chancel was re-paved in 1964; it bears the arms of the St John family who were associated with the church from the 12th century.

14th-century tile

Bishopstone *St Andrew* 40

The spread of urban development from Seaford has not reached Bishopstone which remains separate and quiet in a Downland hollow. Its flint church is remarkable for the amount of pre-Conquest work still existing. The nave and porch (originally a porticus or side chapel) are Saxon; both have stone quoins with typical long and short work. Set into the porch S wall is a sundial incised with a cross and bearing the name EADRIC. The Norman W tower, built in the early 12th century, is in four diminishing stages separated by string courses; a corbel table is carved with heads and grotesques. The chancel (now the choir) was

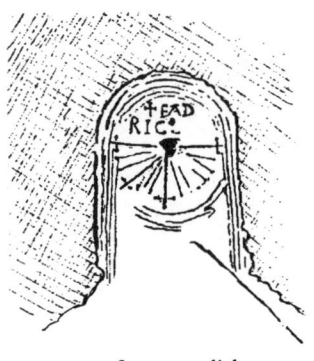

Saxon sundial

rebuilt with wall arcades of semi-circular arches, two moulded and two with chevron ornament. Of later 12th-century date are the N aisle, S doorway to the nave and porch entrance doorway with shafts, carved capitals and double chevron interlacing on the arch. Towards the end of the century the tiny sanctuary was built; its pointed arch has a hoodmould of dogtooth. The arch between nave and choir, with fine mouldings and stiff-leaf capitals, is Early English. The last major alteration to the church was in the 13th century when the aisle arcade was reconstructed. In the tower is a small coffin lid with carved roundels; it dates from the 12th century as does the massive square font.

Bodiam St Giles 72E

The church stands on a wooded hill north of the castle. Most of the fabric dates from the late 14th century; the large blocks of Hastings sandstone in the chancel walls are similar to the masonry of the castle,

18th-century gravestone

built 1385. There was extensive restoration in 1851 and few of the windows are original. The Perpendicular tower is unusual in being oblong, wider from north to south. There is a blocked priest's doorway in the chancel S wall with signs of older foundations beneath. The interior is mainly Victorian but medieval features are the chancel arch, Early English lancets in the chancel S wall, the piscina and double sedilia. On the tower W wall are fragments of memorial brasses including a knight in 14th-century armour and an inscription dated 1513 commemorating a former vicar. The 19th-century font has a tall crocketed cover balanced by a counter weight. In the churchyard are several 18th-century carved gravestones, two of a type commonly seen in Kent with a skull and crossed bones.

Bolney *St Mary Magdalene*

South doorway

Bolney lies half a mile west of the London-Brighton road; its church stands on a steep rise above the village street. The nave and chancel are Norman, built of coursed stone rubble and roofed with Horsham slabs. John Bolney, whose arms are carved on the Perpendicular W doorway, donated the tower in the 16th century. It is built of ashlar and has a parapet with heavy pinnacles. The N aisle and vestry are 19th and 20th-century additions. The most interesting architectural feature is a S doorway of c.1100. Tall and narrow, it has reeded bands around the arch, ornamentation similar to that at Wivelsfield, 5 miles distant. Two small round-headed windows in the chancel date from the 12th century, otherwise the windows are later insertions. The E window has Y-tracery and dates from the 13th century, as does the simple piscina in the S wall. In the nave is a wood panel painted with the Royal Arms of Queen Anne. The fine modern lychgate is built entirely of local materials: Sussex marble, Horsham slabs, oak timbers and stones from a Bolney mill.

Bosham *Holy Trinity*

Saxon tower arch

For many years it was thought that the tower, chancel arch and parts of the walls were from the Saxon church depicted in the Bayeux tapestry but recent research casts doubt on this. Certainly the lower stages of the tower are Saxon (see the tower arch and the doorway above with triangular head). However, the magnificent chancel arch with roll mouldings and cylindrical shafts is now thought to be late 11th or early 12th-century. There are the remains of Norman windows in the chancel, though the E end is early 13th-century, as are the nave and aisles. Particularly fine is the E window, a group of five stepped lancets separated by Purbeck marble shafts; the rear arch too has a set of shafts detached from those of the window. At the E end of the S aisle is a 13th-century crypt with rib-vaulted roof. Of similar date is a two-storeyed sacristy north of the chancel. The font, c.1200, is an octagonal bowl with shallow arcading. In the N aisle is a rare Norman pillar piscina. Tradition maintained that Canute's young daughter was buried beneath the chancel arch and, in an excavation of 1865, a child's coffin of early date was uncovered there.

Botolphs *St Botolph* 10

When the Adur had a wide estuary navigable as far as Bramber, Botolphs was a prosperous place inhabited by people involved in agriculture and shipping. Later the sea receded leaving only a narrow

Jacobean soundboard

river which often flooded and the village declined. Today the ancient church stands almost isolated. Originally an 11th-century building, alterations were made during the 13th century when a N aisle was added to accommodate an increasing population. This was later removed but the three-bay blocked arcade remains. Also of this date is the tower with pyramidal cap, roofed, like the nave, with Horsham slabs. Surviving from the original church are the S walls and one small window at the W end of the nave. The 11th-century round chancel arch has roll moulding and rudimentary decoration on the two responds. The 13th-century chancel, with contemporary piscina and aumbry, has five windows: two lancets (S), one early Decorated (E) and two low side windows (N and S). A Jacobean pulpit and soundboard are decorated with delicate carving. The Royal Arms of Charles II are exhibited at the W end of the church.

Boxgrove *St Mary & St Blaise* 90W

The Benedictine Priory at Boxgrove was demolished at the Dissolution except for the church which was given to the parish. The medieval building did not survive entirely; outside are footings and arcading of the former nave which was largely destroyed, leaving the crossing, N and S transepts and the chancel. These date from three main building periods; the transepts with E and W round arches are c.1120, the Transitional pointed arches of the crossing, supported on pillars with unusual decoration on the capitals, date from c.1170 and from c.1220 is the aisled chancel. The chancel survives completely and is an outstanding example of Early English architecture. Each bay in the arcading has two pointed arches under a wide round arch with a quatrefoil in the spandrel. Above, in the clerestory, are single lancets. Purbeck marble is used extensively for shafts, capitals and even for two pillars; three tall lancets form the beautiful E window. The central vault has ribs ornamented with dogtooth; the delicate foliage painting dates from the 16th century. The magnificent de la Warr chantry chapel, built in 1532, is elaborately carved and has its original iron gate. In the S transept is an early pillar piscina. From the Perpendicular period are the font and a number of tomb chests. In the N aisle is a fine carving on a memorial to the Countess of Derby (d.1752) who is depicted giving alms to the poor.

Early English chancel

Bramber *St Nicholas*

Built soon after the Norman Conquest, the church at Bramber was intended partly as the chapel of the castle. Much of the original cruciform building has gone; the present church has a Norman nave with a tower to the east and a modern vestry at the W end. Arches to the former N and S transepts and a S doorway with billet hoodmould can be seen on the exterior. The tower, formerly the crossing, was restored in 1790 following damage and neglect, since when it has served as the

Early Norman carving

chancel. The upper part with battlemented top is hollow. Of special note inside are the capitals with volutes, heads and animals, rare examples of early Norman carving. On the nave S wall are the Royal Arms of Queen Anne.

Brede *St George* 81E

The village is on high ground above the valley of the river Brede which in Norman times was navigable to the sea. The church dates from the late 12th century though little of the original building remains. The S arcade (round pillars and pointed arches) is of this period; the N arcade (octagonal pillars and double chamfered arches) is 13th-century. In the 15th century the tower was added, the S aisle widened and a new Perpendicular chancel was built. A window above the porch contains fragments of medieval glass. The 15th-century octagonal font is decorated with carved and painted shields. The chapel, which dates from the early 16th century, has carving on the responds of the arch to the chancel and on the outside of the priest's doorway. It contains a tomb recess with brasses commemorating Robert Oxenbregg (d.1482) and his wife. The chapel was built to house the tomb of Sir Goddard Oxenbridge (d.1537); his tomb chest and fine effigy of Caen stone stand near an E window which has tracery in the French Flamboyant style, rare in Sussex. A poor box is carved with churchwardens' initials and the date 1687.

Flamboyant tracery

Brightling *St Thomas à Becket* 62

Brightling is a parish of the High Weald with outstanding views of the Sussex landscape. The 13th-century sandstone church has nave, chancel, N chapel and low W tower. In the 14th century, battlements and massive buttresses were added to the tower. A N aisle was built, at first separate from the chapel, but later joined to it, the junction involving an unusual arrangement of arch and corbel. Decorated windows (two at the E end with reticulated tracery) were added to the Early English lancets. The stone S porch and some nave windows date from the 18th century. Inside the church are remains of wall paintings ranging from 14th-century scrolls to post-Reformation texts. One window contains fragments of 14th-century glass. On the walls are several brasses; the earliest, of the 15th century, has figures of a man and wife and roundels depicting the symbols of St John and St Matthew. In the chapel are memorial slabs and cartouches of the 17th and 18th centuries, all to the Collins family, local ironmasters. A bust set above a marble tablet in the nave commemorates John Fuller, d.1834. 'Mad Jack' Fuller donated the wooden W gallery and the barrel organ that stands in it. His mausoleum is a massive pyramid dominating a corner of the churchyard.

Reticulated tracery

Brighton *St Nicholas* 30

The dark flint church with its prominent golden weathervane stands on a hill above the old town. Nothing remains of the Domesday church; it is not even known if it stood on the present site. The existing church dates from the late 14th century, the nave arcades, the chancel arch and the W tower being of this period. In the 19th century the church was virtually rebuilt with new aisles, chapels and a vestry. The roof was raised and a clerestory added. The many wall memorials were moved to the back of the church where there is also a memorial to the Duke of Wellington in the shape of an Eleanor cross. Windows and wall paintings are the work of Charles Kempe. The chancel screen, restored and repainted, is thought to be 15th-century and perhaps from East Anglia. The great

Norman font

treasure of the church is the Norman font, tub-shaped and carved from a block of Caen stone. Between bands of ornament are various scenes: the Last Supper, the Baptism of Christ and two scenes from the life of St Nicholas of Myra. Pevsner describes it as 'the best piece of Norman carving in Sussex'.

Broadwater St Mary   10

Worthing grew up around the village of Broadwater. St Mary's, one of the largest cruciform churches in the county, was the parish church of the town until 1893. The lower part of the tower remains from an earlier Norman church of the mid 12th century. In the Transitional and Early English periods the church was modified and extended; the belfry stage of the tower and the transepts were added, and the chancel and the large clerestoried, aisled nave built. The E window and N porch are 14th-century. Nave and clerestory windows were replaced in the 15th century. There was a major restoration in the 19th century. Inside, a striking feature is the rich Norman carving on the E and W tower openings: chevron ornament on the arch, bead and beakhead decoration on the soffits.

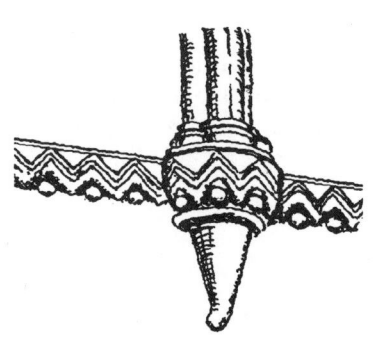

Hook corbel

The chancel has a vaulted stone roof supported by wall shafts resting on hook corbels; around the walls runs a string course of chevron and pellet. At the entrance to the chancel is a low oak screen backed by stalls with carved arms and misericords. Memorials include two 16th-century canopied tomb chests to Lords de la Warr. Among several brasses is one to John Mapilton, a former rector (d.1432), whose vestments have Maple leaf decoration, a play on his name.

Buncton All Saints   11

This tiny Norman chapel, isolated in fields, is situated on the Greensand ridge facing the Downs at Chanctonbury. It probably originated as a chapel served by the monks of Sele Priory but for most of its existence has been joined with a larger parish, at present with

Ashington. The building has a tall narrow nave of the late 11th or early 12th century; small deeply splayed windows high in the N and S walls indicate this date, as do the N (blocked) and S doorways. Embedded in the rubble walls are Roman tiles, possibly from a building that had existed half a mile to the south. The chancel arch is contemporary with the nave, a plain Norman arch of two orders with crude carving including a human figure on the N impost. The chancel too is Norman but was shortened in the 14th century. A new E wall was roughly constructed from squared masonry and rubble and a two-light Decorated E window inserted. The piscina and aumbry are of this date. On the N and S external walls of the chancel are blocks of masonry carved with rich Norman decoration. These appear to be from a larger building, re-used decoratively. The small bellcote was added in the 19th century.

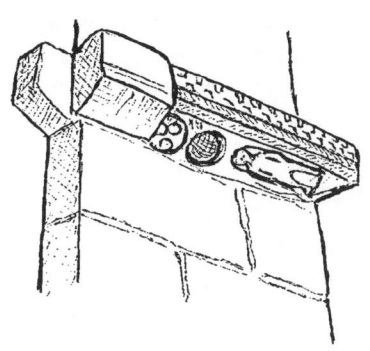

Chancel arch impost

Burpham *St Mary* 00

Burpham is on the east side of the Arun valley at the place where Alfred built a Saxon fort (or Burgh) to protect the area from attack by sea. The church has a Norman nave and N transept, an early 13th-century chancel and a 15th-century W tower. The S transept, aisle and chancel arch are 19th-century rebuildings. It has architectural features of quality. The round arches from nave to transepts show the extremes of Norman style; that to the north is plain with roll moulding over it while the south has zig-zag and deeply cut chevron ornamentation. The pointed arches to the aisle are Transitional with typical moulding and foliage carving. The chancel is vaulted and lit by three deeply splayed lancets

Transept arch

at the E end and 14th-century windows in the N and S walls. A moulded string course around the chancel is typical of the fine architectural detail of the whole building. The octagonal font, deeply carved on bowl and stem, dates from c.1400. Old woodwork includes 15th-century bench ends and the 17th-century communion rail. A churchyard gravestone to a jockey, Benjamin Brewster (d.1789), has a lively carving of racehorse and rider.

Burton 91W

Burton Park is a large 19th-century house under the western Downs. The tiny church, hidden by trees, stands close by. It is of 11th-century date and has Norman herringbone masonry in the N wall. The square-headed mullioned windows were part of the major restoration of 1636, the E window the only visible sign of 19th-century work. The interior is much as it was left in 1636. Between nave and chancel is a 15th-century rood screen and beam, some original colour still visible. The plastered tympanum above has painted commandments from the 17th century and there are other religious texts on the walls. A window splay has a painting of a female martyr, upside down, probably St Uncumber. In the chancel is a canopied tomb recess with the effigy of a lady, possibly 15th-century. Two large 16th-century monuments in the nave commemorate members of the Goring family; on one of these are small inscribed brasses, memorials to later Gorings. The plain tub font must be part of the original Norman church. Dominating the nave are the huge painted Royal Arms of Charles I.

The Royal Arms

Burwash *St Bartholomew* 62

The church was extensively restored in 1856 when the chancel, aisles, vestry and W porch were rebuilt. Parts of the medieval building remain, the oldest being the Norman tower, a substantial structure with walls about 1m thick at the base. Its twin bell-openings have central shafts with scalloped capitals. Above is a shingled broach spire, typical of Sussex. The large W porch leads through the tower into the nave. This has a four-bay Decorated N arcade (1240-50) and an earlier three-bay S arcade. The wide 13th-century chancel arch springs from corbels. A drawing of the church in 1784 shows the rebuilt chancel to be a copy of the former one. The Perpendicular octagonal font has the Pelham buckle carved on two of its concave sides. On the wall of the S aisle are two memorials. One, to Jhone Colins, dates from the 14th century and is thought to be the earliest datable iron graveslab in the country; near it is a brass of an unidentified figure of c.1440. The church possesses a 'Breeches' Bible which is displayed in the tower. On three gravestones in the churchyard are terracotta plaques by Harmer.

Perpendicular font

Bury *St John the Evangelist* 01

Bury, on the river Arun, is the site of an old ferry crossing to Amberley. The church is built of flint and stone rubble with plaster covering most of the exterior. It has a W tower (c.1200) of large dimensions with shingled broach spire, a tall nave with S aisle (12/13th centuries), a S porch (c.1500) and a 19th-century chancel. There are round-headed windows in the tower, narrow lancets in the first two stages and larger openings at belfry level. On the outer wall of the stone porch is a holy water stoup; the inner doorway is Perpendicular with a four-centred arch in a rectangular frame. Dominating the interior are the massive circular pillars of the three-bay arcade which rest on large blocks of rough stone. They have capitals of chalk with stiff-leaf carving and pointed arches of two orders, moulded on the nave side, chamfered on the other.

Porch with holy water stoup

Under the western arch is the 15th-century font, octagonal and carved with rosettes. There is old woodwork; the battlemented rood beam is possibly 13th-century, the well preserved chancel screen is 15th-century and from the 17th century are the pulpit (dated 1628) and the bier hanging in the tower.

Buxted *St Margaret* 42

The 13th-century church in Buxted Park honours Margaret, Queen of Scotland, an uncommon dedication. The village surrounded it until about 1830 when the Lord of the Manor, to gain privacy, relocated Buxted outside the park. The upper part of the W tower is later work; it carries a shingled broach spire and houses eight bells. In the Early English nave are four-bay arcades to N and S aisles. There are clerestory windows (17th-century) on the N side only. Chancel and arch are of the Decorated period; the splendid five-light E window has intersecting cusped tracery. A fine plaster ceiling (c.1600) is decorated with urns containing hop branches (note the two urns upside down) and a marguerite motif also found in the Jacobean pulpit carving. An early 'cross' brass on the chancel floor has the demi-figure of Britellus Avenel, a 14th-century rector. There are triple sedilia and a piscina. The 17th-century communion rail has sturdy, close balusters. A chapel to the south, recently restored, is furnished with a 17th-century altar table and modern chairs made of local wild cherry. The Early English font has arcading and rounded corners; near it is a late 13th-century oak chest carved with rosettes and cusped arches.

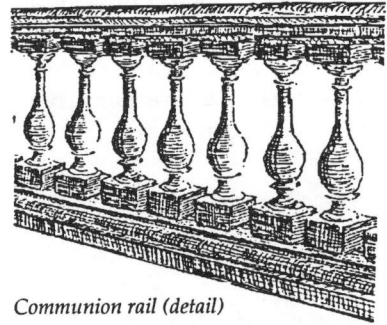
Communion rail (detail)

Catsfield *St Laurence* 71E

The church stands beside the manor, much as it did at the time of the Domesday Survey. Herringbone masonry in the nave S wall indicates an early Norman church; the inner arch of the S doorway, round-headed and tall, is of the same period. The W tower (now with shingled broach spire) was added c.1200. The Early English chancel retains its lancet windows and a 13th-century piscina in the S wall; the E window is modern. Dating from the 14th century are the S and W doorways and the crown-post roof. The N aisle, chapel, vestry and porch are 19th-century additions. Hidden by the organ is a large tapering graveslab with a floriated cross in relief, probably of the 14th century. Above the tower arch is a memorial by Nollekens to John Fuller, erected by his nephew, 'Mad Jack' Fuller of Brightling. Most unusual is the ancient holy water stoup by the S door, set in the jamb and with semi-circular openings giving access from two directions.

Holy water stoup

Chailey *St Peter*

The oldest parts of the church date from the 13th century: the chancel, W tower and, inside, the N arcade. Parts of the S aisle are from the 14th century. Nave, N aisle and vestries are the result of Victorian restoration. The short tower with angle buttresses has a pyramidal shingled spire of about the same height. External medieval features ot the chancel are the lancet windows and the blocked priest's doorway in the S wall. Within, there is fine detail to the chancel windows, framed by rear arches with mouldings and carved capitals, one with a dragon, the rest with stiff-leaf foliage. The Royal Arms in the N aisle are those of Queen Victoria. Among the memorials is an 18th-century iron graveslab in the tower. In the churchyard are many burials marked by 17th or 18th-century gravestones of considerable thickness.

Angle buttresses

Chalvington *St Bartholomew*

St Bartholomew's is only half a mile from the neighbouring church at Ripe. It is a simple flint building with stone quoins and has a chancel, nave with bell turret and a modern porch; the gables of the nave are tile-hung and the turret has a shingled broach spire. The church dates from the late 13th century; the chancel windows of two-light trefoil lancets have unusual flattened hood-moulds on the exterior. The nave windows have simple bar tracery and one (SE) has carved heads on the label stops, as does the N entrance doorway. There is no chancel arch. The three-light E window was added about a century later and contains old glass in the tracery which records in Lombardic script the gift of the window by Thos. Dilywit, rector from 1388 to 1409. A panel of glass in one nave window (NE) depicts an archbishop carrying a crozier and has the inscription S.TH/OM/AS. It dates from c.1300 and is among the oldest in Sussex.

Stained glass panel

Chichester *St Pancras*

No medieval parish church in Chichester survives as a place of worship. All have been deconsecrated and the buildings put to other uses. The only pre-1800 church (apart from the cathedral) is St Pancras'. This was rebuilt completely in 1749 and consisted then of a battlemented W tower, a nave and small chancel, little more than a sanctuary. During a restoration in 1849 a N aisle was added; in 1991 a further N extension provided parish facilities. The exterior is of flint, knapped and squared, with quoins and other stonework in pale grey Portland stone. The windows have been described as a Georgian attempt at

Nave window

pointed Gothic, a forerunner of the Victorian Gothic Revival. Inside there is little to be seen of the 18th-century church. Two nave S windows remain and contain painted glass bearing the names and arms of the benefactors who rebuilt the church. Two circular windows in the N and S walls light the chancel. The 18th-century font was removed in the 1991 reordering of the interior.

Chiddingly 51

Three ancient stone spires remain in Sussex, the oldest at Chiddingly. It surmounts a Perpendicular tower built of local sandstone and finished with polygonal pinnacles. The W doorway has Pelham buckles as label stops. Inside, the high tower arch has semi-octagonal responds. The building dates from the Early English period; the later three-bay nave arcades (probably 14th-century) give onto aisles which retain original lancet windows at the W end. There are old box pews and an 18th-century panelled pulpit. The chancel was rebuilt in the 19th century. A huge alabaster monument in the S transept is to Sir John Jefferay (d.1578) who built the nearby mansion, Chiddingly Place. His effigy reclines high above that of his wife; figures of members of his family stand in niches on either side

The Jefferay monument

and a daughter kneels below. Other memorials to the Jefferay family include a 17th-century wall tablet with kneeling figures. Set into the floor of nave and chancel are 17th and 18th-century ledger slabs. In the churchyard, near the N porch, a gravestone has a Harmer terracotta plaque and on the S side is a wooden graveboard.

Chidham 70W

A mile west of Bosham, across an inlet of Chichester Harbour, is the quiet hamlet of Chidham. Its small church has a 13th-century nave and chancel; the short N aisle was added in the 14th century. A sympathetic restoration in 1864 kept its simple character, the only

Aisle window

modern addition being the large buttressed bellcote. The flint walls with ashlar dressings have mainly lancet windows; some, including the triplet E window are modern, others as in the chancel S wall are 13th-century. Inside, the two-bay arcade has double-chamfered arches on an octagonal pillar and abacus. The aisle windows are of two stepped lancets with trefoil heads. A square opening on the nave N wall gave access to a former rood loft. The chancel arch of two orders was enlarged in the 19th century incorporating the original stones. In the chancel is a 13th-century trefoil-headed piscina and a low recess to the east of uncertain date and purpose. Two early 18th-century cartouches on the S wall have designs incorporating cherubs, skulls and strapwork.

Chithurst   82W

If the modern additions (porch, bellcote and S buttress) are discounted, the church appears much as it did in the 11th century and is probably

Ancient graveslabs

the ecclesiola or little chapel mentioned in Domesday Book. The tall narrow walls of nave and chancel are built of rubble and plastered and there is herringbone work on the N side. Alterations came two centuries later when larger windows were inserted, including the E window of two cusped lights. A small 11th-century window remains on the N side of the chancel. South of the altar is a 13th-century piscina. The plain chancel arch is early Norman; to the north is a squint of later date. In the nave S wall near the W end is a 14th-century two-light window with quatrefoil above, copied in the 19th century further east. Some of the wooden benches with narrow seats are Jacobean. The tub-shaped font is 12th-century. Along the path in the churchyard are ancient graveslabs (possibly 11th/12th-century). Below the mound (probably artificial) on which the church is built, flows the river Rother.

Clapham *St Mary* 00

A narrow lane from the village leads to the church near the edge of Clapham woods. Though originally a Norman building, the present church is mainly of the 13th century. It consists of a nave with aisles, a chancel inclining noticeably to the north and a low NW tower. The nave arcades differ in age and style. That on the north, of two bays, has capitals with foliage carving; a blocked Norman arch above is from the earlier church. The later three-bay S arcade is typically Early English. Both aisles have 15th-century two-light windows. The chancel arch and lancet windows were restored in the 19th century. There are memorials to members of the Michelgrove and Shelley families, former Lords of the Manor. A brass on the floor to John Shelley (d.1526) and his wife has shells of the Shelley arms (a pun on the name) on his tabard. A canopied tomb recess (N wall) is to William Shelley (d.1548) and his wife who kneel with their fourteen children. An early graveslab with a foliated cross is preserved in the N aisle.

Canopied tomb recess

Clayton *St John* 21

The hamlet of Clayton lies at the foot of the Downs eight miles north of Brighton. Its church, recorded in Domesday Book, has a small chancel and lofty nave with a shingled bell turret. In the flint walls are traces of arches to former transeptal chapels. A ripplestone churchyard path leads to the N entrance porch and a Norman doorway. There is an ancient door with moulded back rails and an oak lock. The fine 11th-century chancel arch has bold half-round moulding and massive chamfered imposts, a solid and powerful design. Even more impressive are the remarkable wall paintings dating from c.1100 which

Christ Enthroned

were discovered at the end of the 19th century. They are part of the 'Lewes Group' of paintings (which include those at Coombes, Hardham, and Plumpton) created by a single workshop, possibly associated with Lewes Priory. The paintings depict the Last Judgement proclaimed by four angels blowing trumpets. Over the chancel arch is the figure of Christ Enthroned with apostles standing on either side. On the N wall, bishops, kings and laymen process towards St Peter and the Heavenly City. On the S wall a spike-heeled devil riding a large beast separates the doomed from the blessed.

Climping *St Mary* 00

Climping, across the river from Littlehampton, has a large 13th-century parish church consisting of nave with S aisle, chancel and transepts. At the end of the S transept is an earlier tower (c.1170) with ornament of the late Norman period, some of the best in Sussex; zig-zag and deeply cut chevron carving decorate the narrow windows and the W doorway. The church was built c.1220 in the Early English style and it is the fine proportions and elegant simplicity that perhaps make the greatest impression. Windows are tall lancets with, on the end walls, a circular opening above; the E window is of three lancets of equal height, though of slightly different width. The S arcade has round pillars with moulded capitals and bases with spurs; the arches have elaborate moulding rather than simple chamfers. Much of the building is in Caen stone and the workmanship is of high quality. There is good detail everywhere, in the corbels to

Tower doorway

aisle and transept, in the matching piscina and aumbry in the chancel and in the rear arches and nook shafts of the E window. St Mary's has one of the two medieval stone pulpits in Sussex (14th-century), an octagonal font of similar date, 15th-century bench ends and an exceptional 13th-century chest.

Coates *St Agatha* 91W

The tiny church of St Agatha stands above the narrow lane through Coates, a hamlet with a few cottages and a small manor house. Built of local stone, its Norman origin is evident in the thick walls of nave and chancel. A later N vestry is of unknown date; the wooden bell turret is a recent replacement. In the 16th century the N doorway was enlarged and the timber porch constructed. Typical of that period is the door itself, of double oak planks arranged vertically outside and horizontally within. In the white plastered interior the Norman chancel arch, plain with chamfered imposts, is big and impressive in so small a church. One original window remains high up in the S wall; the Early English lancets were inserted in the 13th century with, uncommonly, two rather than three at the E end. From the same period are the crude sedile (chancel S wall) and the holy water stoup (nave N wall). The roof has six tie-beams, two with queen-posts supporting the bell turret. The square Norman font, one side set into the W wall, is carved with round-headed arches.

16th-century door

Cocking 81W

A church at Cochinges, recorded in the Domesday Book, was replaced by the present Norman building consisting of a simple nave and chancel to which a S aisle and W tower were added in the 14th century. The N aisle, vestry and S porch are modern. The three-stage tower, built of local malmstone (plastered), has two-light belfry windows and a pyramidal roof. The porch leads into the S aisle which has two Decorated windows, one with a cinquefoil niche on each side;

Wall painting

in the S wall are an aumbry and a piscina. Above the two-bay arcade is a small round-headed Norman window; a medieval Nativity painting in the splay shows an angel appearing to two shepherds with a dog. This window, blocked when the aisle was constructed, was discovered in the 19th century. The low chancel arch and traces of windows in the chancel are Norman. A piscina in the S wall and a recessed tomb (N) with an ogee arch and carved heads, date from the 14th century. To the east is part of a graveslab with a Y-shaped cross; this was found in the chancel foundations and may be pre-Conquest. The 12th-century font is plain and tub-shaped.

Coldwaltham St Giles

The oldest part of the church is the Norman tower with thick walls and short clasping buttresses. Below its pyramidal cap is an unusual half-timbered top. During a major 19th-century restoration, a N aisle and vestry were added to the existing small church. Inside, a 13th-century arcade separates the nave and S aisle; this has two bays of unequal width with a central pier and chamfered arches dying into the imposts. In the chancel S wall are Decorated windows, a 13th-century piscina and a priest's doorway which was uncovered in recent times. Most furnishings are 19th-century, though many of the oak pews with deep moulded tops date from the 18th century. The bowl-shaped font is Norman and stands in the tower; the plain Transitional tower arch to the nave is c.1200. Near it is a narrow graveslab, possibly of even earlier date, approximately 30cm thick and carved with a cross. Also of great

Decorated window

age is the churchyard yew with a girth of 9-10 m., one of the oldest in the country.

Compton *St Mary* 71W

Compton is a pre-Conquest village at the western edge of the Sussex Downs with its parish bordering onto Hampshire. The Domesday Book records a church here but little of an ancient church remains. The main structure is a 19th-century rebuilding in flint with stone quoins, consisting of nave, chancel, S aisle, N porch and vestry and a small bellcote with a shingled spire. The flint work shows rough galleting, the insertion of flint chips in the mortar between the large flints of the wall. In the N wall of the nave are the remains of a blocked Norman arcade with round-headed arches and a capital with water-leaf decoration. The chancel arch is of similar 12th-century date but has the Transitional pointed shape. The S arcade is mainly 13th-century. A medieval aumbry and piscina are incorporated in the modern chancel.

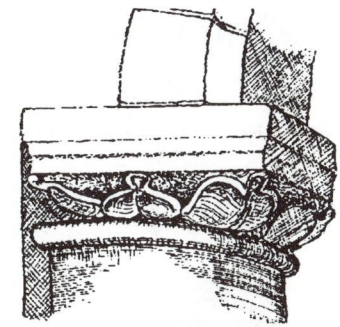

Waterleaf decoration

Coombes 10

Coombes was once a small village but now is no more than a farm and a few houses. The lovely church is small and unrestored; its W end cuts into the slope of the Downs, its E end faces the flood plain of the river Adur. The nave, S doorway and chancel arch remain from the 11th century early Norman church. The chancel was rebuilt in the 13/14th centuries. Perpendicular windows were inserted in the S wall in the 15th century; fragments of glass and floor tiles of this period can still be seen. The E window and porch date

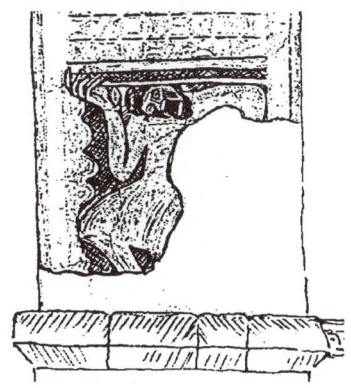

Chancel arch painting

from the 16th century. In the 18th century the W end was rebuilt and the bell turret added. Wall paintings of several periods were uncovered in 1949. The most extensive and interesting, like those at Clayton and Hardham, date from c.1100: Christ in Majesty above the chancel arch, scenes from a Nativity cycle on the N and S walls. On the underside of the chancel arch is a grimacing, Herculean figure straining under the weight of the masonry above.

Cowfold *St Peter* 22

Cowfold church is built of brown Wealden sandstone under Horsham slab roofs. The oldest parts are the chancel and N wall of the nave.

St Pancras
The Nelond brass (detail)

There are three 13th-century lancet windows in the chancel N wall, one containing a small stained glass crucifixion of the 14th century. Blocked lancets are visible in the chancel S and nave N walls. The stout W tower, added in the 15th century, is of ashlar with battlemented top, a pyramidal cap of Horsham stone and a higher stair turret. Built during the 16th century were the arcade with four-centred arches and the S aisle with flat headed windows under internal segmental arches. Records date the font to 1481. The great treasure of the church is a large brass of Thomas Nelond, Prior of Lewes (1433), which must have been removed from the Priory of St Pancras at the Dissolution. Picturesque cottages surround the churchyard which has memorials noteworthy for their variety of form and carving.

Crawley *St John the Baptist* 23

The medieval church of a small market town is now surrounded by the car parks and commerce of Crawley New Town. Originally St John's was a 13th-century chapel of nave and chancel; part of this exists in the stone rubble of the nave S wall. In the 15th century the three-stage W tower of sandstone ashlar was added; the nave was heightened (the later stone is clearly visible above the old wall) and covered with a new roof of Horsham slabs. In the 19th century the N aisle was added, a new chancel built and the tower raised. Three medieval figure carvings have been set in the W wall, the uppermost thought to represent St John. Entrance is through the tower into the long nave with its seven-bay arcade. The fine 15th-century roof has moulded wall plates and tie-beams, rafters with arch-braced collars and purlins with wind braces; one tie-beam carries an inscription in Gothic lettering. In 1990 the E end of the church was rearranged. The altar was moved forward to the chancel arch and backed by a new wooden screen. The chancel became the Lady chapel; two brasses of the 15th and 16th centuries are reset in the floor. The Jacobean communion rail with twisted balusters now surrounds the organ.

15th-century roof

Crowborough *All Saints* 53

Until the coming of the railway in the 19th century, Crowborough was a small scattered community in Rotherfield parish. In 1744 All Saints' was built as a chapel of Rotherfield church by a local landowner and benefactor, Sir Henry Fermor; his name and the date are inscribed above the W door. Drawings in the Burrell and Sharpe collections show the building c.1800. The present tower is all that is left of this church; it is built of ashlar and has a square-headed doorway, circular openings housing clock faces at belfry level, battlements and a sharply pointed, shingled octagonal spire. In 1881 the church was enlarged to meet the needs of the increased population. Unlike most Victorian churches, this is in a restrained classical style: arcades of round arches with crocketed capitals, round-headed two-light windows and an apsidal E end.

18th-century tower

Crowhurst St George 71E

Crowhurst lies two miles north west of Hastings. To the south of the church are the ruins of the 14th-century manor and what is reputed to be the largest churchyard yew in Sussex. The W tower was built by the Pelham family in the 15th century; it has a W door with a three-light Perpendicular window above, diagonal buttresses and a battlemented top. The label stops on the doorway arch take the form of the Pelham buckle. Apart from the tower, the church dates from the 19th century; nave, N aisle, chancel and vestry were built by Teulon in 14th-century style. In the churchyard are early 18th-century gravestones of dark stone, typically low and thick.

18th-century gravestones

Cuckfield Holy Trinity 32

Although close to Haywards Heath, Cuckfield preserves its village identity. Only the foundations of a Norman church remain. The earliest parts of the present building, S aisle and lower tower, are 13th-century. The rest is mainly 14th-century work: the N aisle, N and S chapels and clerestory. The tower was heightened and finished with a trefoil-headed frieze, battlements and a slender recessed spire. In the 15th century the church was re-roofed in a single span, concealing the clerestory windows which were uncovered in recent times. A notable interior feature is the 15th-century oak wagon roof with carved bosses and moulded tie-beams on traceried spandrels. C.E.Kempe painted the roof in the 19th century. Of the many fine memorials, several are to members of the Burrell family; the earliest is a brass to

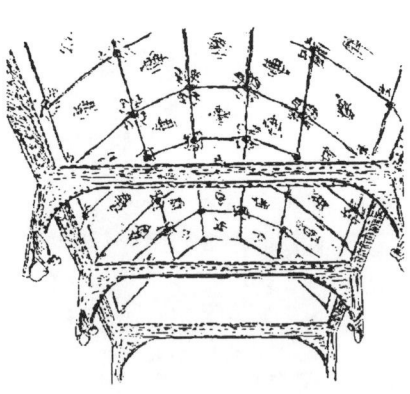
Wagon roof

Gerard Borell (d.1509), a former vicar, and the most recent to Percy Burrell who died in battle (1810), an event depicted in sculpture. Others commemorate the Sergisons who owned Cuckfield Park. A large baroque sculpture by Thomas Adye has the seated figure of Truth holding a portrait of Charles Sergison (d.1732) in full bottomed wig. The tub-shaped font (restored) is 13th-century. From the churchyard, which has 17th and 18th-century gravestones, are extensive views to the Downs.

Dallington *St Giles* 61

Rectors of Dallington are recorded from the 13th century but no building of that time remains. Except for the W tower, the church was demolished in 1864 and replaced by the present Victorian building in the Gothic style. The 15th-century Perpendicular tower, built of sandstone, has angle buttresses and is of three storeys with a NE stair turret. It is one of several Pelham towers in Sussex; carved on the battlemented parapet are the family arms (a shield with three pelicans) and the badge (the Pelham buckle). The moulded W doorway is under a square label with roses carved in the spandrels; above is a large three-light window. Crowning the tower is a stone spire, one of only three in Sussex of medieval date, the others being at Chiddingly and Northiam. The octagonal font, probably coeval with the tower, has concave sides decorated with a variety of carvings. All the memorials were removed when the church was demolished but in recent years several 18th-century wall tablets were found in the belfry and these are mounted on the N wall.

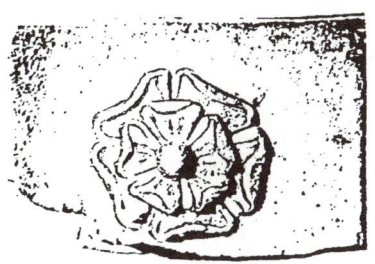

Font carving

Denton *St Leonard* 40

Denton is another Downland village engulfed by urban development, in this case from Newhaven. The church of flint and sandstone dates from the 13th century. In the 19th century the chancel roof was raised so that the whole structure is now tiled with a roof line unbroken apart

Norman font

from a small bell turret. Originally a rood screen separated nave from chancel (the stairway to the rood loft remains in the S wall) but now the interior is one large chamber. The windows include 13th-century lancets and some of 14th-century Geometrical style. The four-light E window shows a variation of Decorated intersecting tracery. It is filled with 19th-century stained glass by Kempe with angels in the tracery lights. The fine sedile and piscina, also 14th-century, have cusped arches. A large Norman font has a carved bowl with basket weave decoration similar to that at St Anne's, Lewes.

Didling St Andrew   81W

Didling, a farm and a few houses, is a small community in the far west of the county. The church, alone in fields, is on the lower slopes of the Downs to the south. It has a small 13th-century nave and chancel in a single room, a modern N porch and bellcote. In the 14th century the chancel S wall was rebuilt; the E and W walls have been repaired in brick. St Andrew's has an unspoilt interior with the simplicity of a farm building. The doorway has a low flat lintel. The walls and ceiled rafters are whitewashed. Two Early English lancets in deep splays form the E window. In the chancel N wall are two lancets under segmental heads; the 14th-century windows in the S wall have pointed trefoil heads. There is a Jacobean communion rail; the pulpit was made from a 17th-century church chest. The font, 12th-century or earlier, is tub-shaped, roughly finished, on a round base. Contributing most of all to the character of the church are the medieval benches, thick blackened oak with rough rounded ends, described in Pevsner as 'village woodwork'.

Medieval benches

Ditchling *St Margaret*

St Margaret's is a large cruciform church set on a high point in the centre of the village. It has a nave of the 11/12th centuries with a simple Transitional arcade to a S aisle. The tower (with a low shingled spire), the chancel and S transept are of the late 13th century. The N transept was built during the Victorian restoration and houses the organ. Especially fine is the ornate Early English stonework (Caen stone and chalk) of the tower arches and chancel. The chancel E window is in the Geometrical style, three lancets surmounted by three foiled circles, the hoodmould with royal heads as label stops. Slender shafts with foliage capitals separate the lights; similar shafts and carving are found on the lancets of the N wall. In the S wall are piscina and sedile under pointed arches. The pillars of the crossing show

Foliage capital and label stop

a variety of decoration: stiff-leaf capitals to the east, simpler moulded capitals to the west. The early 14th-century S chapel has a fine Decorated window with reticulated tracery and contains an Elizabethan memorial to Henry Poole d. 1580.

Donnington *St George*

The church stands by itself west of the Chichester–Selsey Road. Of 13th-century date are the chancel, nave and aisles. The battlemented tower was added in the 16th century, the upper floors reached by the original ladder of triangular wooden blocks. Following a fire in 1939 the nave and aisles were extensively restored. Over the chancel arch are the Royal Arms of George III. The chancel windows are deeply splayed lancets; the E wall has a triplet with moulded jambs and a continuous hoodmould. A string course runs at sill height

Piscina

round the three walls. In the S wall is a piscina with a double drain and trefoil head. The N chapel was rebuilt in the 19th century; it contains memorials to the Crosbie family including two busts of c.1840. An elegant monument to John Page (d.1779) takes the form of a sarcophagus, surmounted by an urn, with Ionic columns and a frieze of palm and oak branches. The church's furnishings are modern, although old panelling is incorporated in the pulpit.

Earnley   89W

Earnley, a group of houses and a farm, is on the Selsey Peninsula a mile inland from the sea. Its simple church stands in a narrow triangular churchyard within flint walls and consists of nave and chancel of equal width, a bell turret (tiled and shingled) and a modern N porch. The exterior walls of stone rubble contain a variety of materials, some apparently from the seashore. Entrance to the 13th-century nave is through the old N doorway; the nave windows are modern replacements. A wooden arch opens into the 14th-century chancel with aumbry, piscina and windows of this date; the two-light E window has trefoil heads and a quatrefoil above, the single-light N and S windows have cusped trefoil heads. In the churchyard is the grave of a soldier who was awarded the Victoria Cross.

14th-century window

Eartham St Margaret   90W

Eartham is a quiet Downland village near Chichester. The church was extensively restored in 1869 and the Victorian exterior masks its 12th-century origins. A modern porch shelters a Norman W doorway, tall with plain jambs; a stone lintel and the arch above form a tympanum which is filled with ashlar. Also Norman is the large and impressive chancel arch of two orders. It rests on shafts with volute capitals which have small carvings of a bearded man and the head of a hare. The flanking openings are modern. In the 13th century the chancel was rebuilt and the S aisle was added. The two-bay nave arcade has pointed arches and a central round pillar with moulded base and capital. All windows, except for the inner jambs of the E lancet, are 19th-century as are the furnishings and roof timbers; a tile in the chancel floor shows the Royal Arms of Queen Victoria. On the N wall is a 17th-century memorial to the daughters of a former vicar. A monument in the nave to poet Thomas Hayley (d.1800), with an angel holding a wreath, is by Flaxman.

Chancel arch capital

Easebourne *St Mary* 82W

Part of the 11th-century church at Easebourne became a Priory church in the 13th century when an order of Benedictine nuns was established there. The Parish kept the western end and the N aisle, which was widened to form a new nave. Until the Dissolution in 1535 the two churches functioned side by side. The W tower dates from the late 12th century as does the western part of the arcade (one and a half bays), spared when much of the church was rebuilt during a major 19th-century restoration. In the 11th-century S wall can be seen the arch of a Norman doorway. Also Norman is the Purbeck marble font, a square bowl with arcading on three sides. In a 13th-century recess (N wall) is the alabaster effigy of Sir David Owen (d.1535) in armour of the period. The elaborate marble and alabaster monument to Anthony, Viscount Montague (d.1592) and his two wives was brought from Midhurst in the 19th century and stands at the E end of the chapel. It suffered damage in the move and was rearranged to fit its present position; a drawing of 1780 by Grimm shows the monument in its original and complete form.

Montague monument (detail)

East Blatchington *St Peter* 49

The former Downland village of East Blatchington is now surrounded by housing development from Seaford; its church has 12th-century origins and part of the existing nave walls are of this period. The Norman church had a central tower which was replaced in the 13th century by the present W tower. This has string courses and lancet openings at the belfry stage and carries a shingled broach spire. Occasional large brown sarsen stones are incorporated in the fabric of the church which is mainly of flint with stone quoins. The long nave (originally the Norman nave and tower) has a crown-post roof with old tie-beams. Divided from the nave by a high, wide arch is the Early English chancel. It has lancet windows and, in the S wall, a trefoil-headed piscina and double sedilia with a Purbeck marble shaft. To the west is the earliest feature in the church, the priest's doorway, round-headed with one plain chamfer. The modern baptistery is attractively sited in the tower.

Priest's doorway

Eastbourne *St Mary* 69

St Mary's stands alongside the High Street in Eastbourne Old Town, about a mile inland. The large 12th-century building of flint and stone has chancel and nave with clerestory and aisles. In the 14th century the church was enlarged when the green sandstone tower was added, aisles widened and the unusual vestry against the E wall was built. On each side of the modern E window is a 13th-century window with Geometrical tracery. The interior is a notable example of Transitional work in Caen stone. Arcades in nave and chancel have pointed arches, alternate round and octagonal pillars and capitals with stiff-leaf carving. The westernmost bays and the

Piscina and sedilia

square font are contemporary with the tower which has barrel vaulting and a Perpendicular window. Also of 14th-century date are the piscina, triple sedilia and Easter Sepulchre in the chancel and the wooden parclose screens enclosing the chapels. Although the rood loft has gone, a rare rood piscina remains on the nave S wall. There are three hatchments and the painted Royal Arms of George III. In the S aisle is a memorial to Henry Lushington (d.1763) with a bust and a graphic account of the last years of his life.

East Chiltington   31

From 1291 until 1909 the church was a chapel of ease to Westmeston, after which it became a parish church. The nave is Norman and has original features: the S doorway, a (blocked) N doorway and a small round-headed window in the S wall. At the W end is a low tower of the 13th century with lancet windows and a Sussex cap. The church was restored in the 19th century; the E window and chancel arch are modern. There are 18th-century commandment tablets above the chancel arch and charity boards in the tower, one charity being for 'the lame, aged and impotent people ... of Chiltington'. The pulpit is dated 1719. The church walls are built of local sandstone rubble, weathered brown and encrusted with white lichen.

Charity board

East Dean (East Sussex)   *St Simon & St Jude*   59

East Dean village, midway between Eastbourne and Seaford, shelters in a Downland hollow two miles from the coast. The church is a mixture of medieval and modern building. The oldest part is the tower which may date from the late 11th century and originally formed the nave of an early church. An arch (now blocked) in the E wall led to an apse where the altar stood. The present nave to the south was built in the late 12th century, followed soon afterwards by the chancel which

Jacobean pulpit

has a pronounced inclination to the north. In the 19th century the nave was lengthened; the baptistery was added in 1960. The font is modern, though a Norman fragment is incorporated in the bowl and this provided the basis for its design. In the crown-post nave roof are massive old tie-beams. The carved Jacobean pulpit with back panel and sounding board carries its date, 1623, beneath the ledge. In a corner of the churchyard (NE) are memorials to two unidentified merchant seamen washed ashore in World War II; the inscriptions read: 'Known unto God'.

East Dean (West Sussex) *All Saints*   91W

The church at East Dean, in the Lavant valley near Chichester, stands on rising ground at the N end of the village. This is a cruciform building dating from the 12th century with work from the 13th and 14th centuries in its structure. The battlemented tower with single and twin bell-openings once had a broach spire, as seen in a drawing in the Sharpe collection. Visible in the nave N wall are the arches of an arcade to a former N aisle; a fine architectural detail is the S doorway (c.1200) with roll mouldings and jamb shafts. The crossing arches are round except for one (W) which is segmental. In a major 19th-century restoration the entire E wall was rebuilt, the S porch was added and many windows were replaced. However, the original cruciform plan of central tower between nave and chancel and N and S transepts remains. The octagonal font, thought to be c.1600, has an intriguing base which may be an inverted 12th-century capital brought from elsewhere.

Sussex marble gravestone

Set into the exterior S transept wall is the Sussex marble gravestone of William Peachey (d.1688), a local blacksmith.

Eastergate *St George* 90W

St George's, four miles south west of Arundel, is a church within a farmyard. (Manor Farm is a fine timber-framed building, c.1600, with an old granary on staddlestones.) The church of chancel and aisleless nave was built soon after the Conquest; in the chancel S wall is herringbone work in Roman brick, indicative of the early Norman period, and in the N wall, high up, is a tiny round-headed window of similar age. There is a small bell turret at the W end and a modern vestry north of the nave. A feature of the church is the variety of window styles. Besides the early Norman window with its internal splay, there are two Early English lancets in the chancel S wall.

Chancel window

The nave windows are 14th-century (cinquefoil lights with an opening above) and the E window is 15th-century Perpendicular. The W window of three lights with rounded heads was donated under the terms of a will of 1534. In one nave window (S) is a rare piece of armorial stained glass c.1360. A modern tapestry commemorates the 900th anniversary of the Domesday Survey which says '(Easter)Gate ... here is a church'.

East Grinstead *St Swithun* ✓ 33

Few churches were built in the 18th century; St Swithun's is one of only four in Sussex. Designed by James Wyatt in the Perpendicular style, it was a forerunner of the 19th-century Gothic Revival. It is stone built with a tall W tower (dated 1789), an aisled nave of five bays and a small sanctuary. The E bay of the nave and the sanctuary now form a chancel. There is a clerestory with round windows that have recently been filled with stained glass. The concave

Hatchment

pillars and capitals are reminiscent of the crossing at Alfriston. Some memorials from the former medieval church have been reset: a wall-mounted brass of c.1500 and several cast iron graveslabs including the oldest dated example in the country (1570). Heraldry is much in evidence: 18th-century hatchments on the walls and 20th-century shields of arms on the pew ends.

East Guldeford *St Mary* 92E

St Mary's stands on the edge of Romney Marsh near Rye; the land was reclaimed from the sea in the 15th century by Sir Robert Guldeford who was granted a faculty to build the church. Consecrated in 1505, it is built of bricks varying in colour and laid in English bond; about one metre from the ground a string course of moulded bricks runs round the building and its original buttresses. There is a double roof (18th-century) with a bell turret between. Inside is a plain rectangular space; one roof beam has spandrels with pierced trefoils indicating the division between nave and chancel. Box pews and a two-decker pulpit date from the late 18th/early 19th century. Brought from elsewhere is the 12th-century Sussex marble font. The four-light E window has intersecting tracery. On either side are angel corbels; others are in the N and S walls and each side of the altar. On the sanctuary walls are colourful figures of angels holding musical instruments and other objects; the date of painting is uncertain. The Royal Arms of George IV hang in the nave and a plaque on the N wall carries the Guldeford arms, commemorating the builder of the church.

View from the west

East Hoathly 51

At the W end of the church is a Perpendicular 'Pelham tower' built of sandstone ashlar with diagonal W buttresses. It has a stair turret higher than the battlements and is finished with a spirelet and weathervane. The W doorway, square-headed, has shields and foliage in the spandrels; the label stops are carved in the shape of the Pelham buckle. The tower arch, typically, is very tall and has semi-octagonal responds and capitals. The rest of the church (nave, chancel, aisles and N vestry) was rebuilt in the 19th century. In the chancel is a rare Norman pillar piscina with chevron ornament on the shaft. A ledger slab and wall tablet of the 18th century are from the former church. Later additions include an iron screen to the vestry and a mosaic and painted wall behind the altar. The churchyard contains interesting memorials: a Harmer terracotta plaque and carved gravestones of the 18th century including one to Thomas Turner, the Sussex diarist.

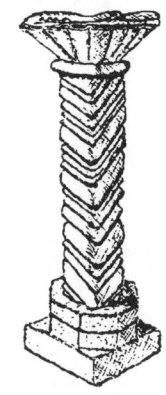

Pillar piscina

East Lavant *St Mary* 80W

The Lavant stream rises near East Dean and flows south past Mid and East Lavant before crossing Chichester to the sea. The nave of St Mary's dates from the 12th century; the W doorway has nook shafts with scalloped capitals and a round arch with chevron and roll moulding decoration. Its 13th-century N aisle was largely replaced in the 19th century when the chancel was completely rebuilt and vestries added. The S tower, chalk with brick facing, dates from 1671, (see the inscribed brass in the tower). Inside, the nave has four-bay arcades; only the two middle arches date from the 13th century, the others are Victorian. Under the tower is a 14th-century tomb recess with cusped segmental arch, reset from the former chancel. A

West doorway

set of five stalls with carved misericords in the chancel is probably 15th-century. The Royal Arms in the nave are those of the Stuart kings. In the N aisle floor are two ancient tapering graveslabs with raised floriated crosses. One, of Sussex marble, has an inscription in Norman French: PRIEZ QI PASSEZ PAR ICI PUR L'ALME LUCI DE MILDEBI.

East Lavington *St Peter* 91W

The parish church of East Lavington (also known as Woolavington) is at the foot of the western Downs, close by Lavington Park. The house is now Seaford College, the church its chapel. This consists of chancel and nave with a N aisle and S transept; a small bellcote sits above the W end. It was extensively restored in the 19th century by G.E.Street obscuring much of the original Early English work. The N arcade of one narrow and two wide double-chamfered arches is ancient as are the rectangular pier and octagonal pillar. Corbels and shafts supporting the inner order of the arches are typical of the 13th century. The wide chancel arch is of similar design. Although all the windows have been replaced, the rear arches appear to be original. Among the furnishings are an elaborately carved pulpit of blackened oak, a modern light oak screen and seats with carved misericords. In the transept is the crozier of Bishop Wilberforce (see Graffham) who is buried in the churchyard.

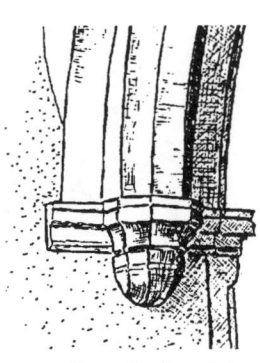
Chancel arch corbel

East Marden 81W

East Marden's Early English church stands above the narrow road through the village with its picturesque thatched well-head. The main structure is of flint rubble with ashlar dressings under a tiled roof. A bell turret has boarded sides and its pyramidal roof is also tiled. The 17th-century S porch leads to a 13th-century interior, simple and unadorned. Nave and chancel, with no division between, have ancient tie-beams. The E window is a triple lancet and other lancets in the N and S walls are original. The 13th-century N doorway with pointed arch now gives access to the modern vestry. There is a goblet-

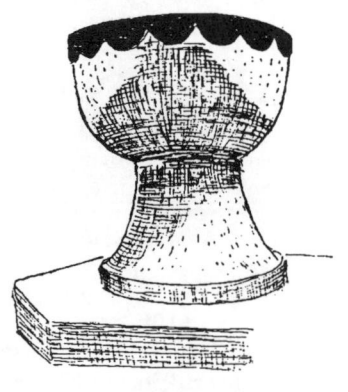
Norman font

shaped lead-lined font, probably 12th-century. On the walls are two 18th-century memorial tablets, one from an affectionate grandson to his grandparents 'in whose house he was bred up'.

East Preston *St Mary* 00

The earliest part of East Preston church is the N doorway which survives from the original 12th-century Norman nave. There is no structural division between nave and the 13th-century chancel. The narrow Perpendicular tower with a N stair turret was added c.1500 and until 1951 had a stone spire. The porch, S aisle and vestry are modern. An impressive feature inside the church is the high tower arch of Pulborough sandstone with continuous mouldings. There are lancet and two-light Perpendicular windows and a notable Early English E window of three lancets, the central one slightly larger, separated by Purbeck marble shafts with stiff-leaf capitals. There are old pews (with renewed seats) at the W end of the nave; the oak entrance door has an old wooden lockcase.

Wooden lockcase

Edburton *St Andrew*   21

St Andrew's situation is memorable; the steep slope of the Downs rises immediately to the south and from the churchyard are extensive views across the Weald. There is evidence of an earlier church; some of its stones were re-used in the present 13th-century building. Four mass dials can be found in the walls. The substantial W tower of coursed flint has a Sussex cap. The S porch, roofed mainly with Horsham stone, leads into a broad, aisleless nave with lancet windows. It has a crown-post roof and moulded tie-beams with billet decoration. The

Lead font

two-light windows of the N chapel (originally a chantry chapel) and the E window of the chancel contain unusual 19th-century stained glass made in Munich. There are two small low side windows in the N and S chancel walls. The lead font, one of only three in Sussex, is circular and decorated with scrolls and arcades. Archbishop Laud donated the Jacobean pulpit and carved communion rail.

Egdean St Bartholomew   92W

Egdean, sometimes known as Bleatham, is a small place a mile or so SE of Petworth. The old church became ruinous c.1547 during the reign of Edward VI; a new one was built in 1622. A drawing in the Sharpe collection shows how it appeared in 1805: a small buttressed nave and chancel, mainly of stone rubble but with quoins, window surrounds and S doorway of brick. Restoration in the 19th and 20th centuries replaced most of the windows and added a bellcote, S porch and N vestry but otherwise the church exterior is as in the drawing: the brick doorway bears the date 1622, one small brick window remains in the W wall, the quoins are of small 17th-century bricks and the kneestones and coping of the E gable are probably original. Inside there is more brickwork: the wide round-headed chancel arch and the rear arches of the chancel windows. There are old tie-beams, one dated 1623. The communion rail, a small inscribed brass and the plain octagonal font also date from the seventeenth century. In the churchyard are 18th-century carved gravestones.

18th-century gravestone

Elsted St Paul   81W

Elsted, beneath the Downs in the west of the county, had a church recorded in the Domesday Book. The walls of this 11th-century building can be seen in the present nave, the best example of herringbone masonry in Sussex. In the 12th century a N aisle and chancel were added but all that remains is the blocked arcade in the N wall and the plain Norman chancel arch. The chancel was replaced in the 13th century and is essentially the one seen today. It has two Early English lancets in the E wall and similar lancets in N and S walls; there is a moulded string course. At the end of the 19th century the church was in a ruinous condition; only nave walls and chancel remained. The church at Treyford became the parish church but by 1947 this too was in disrepair and was demolished. St Paul's was then restored; the nave walls were built up, clerestory windows added in the S wall, new W windows inserted, the nave re-roofed and a vestry built in the position of a S aisle. It was re-dedicated in 1951.

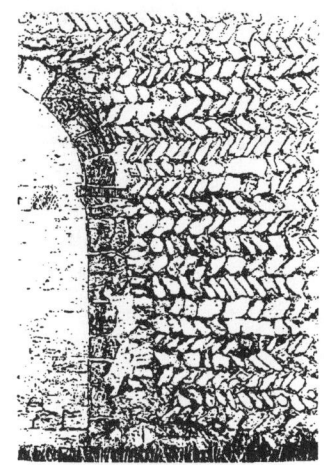

Herringbone masonry

Etchingham   *The Assumption & St Nicholas*   72E

The church was built of Hastings sandstone about 1366/69 and is entirely in the late Decorated style. It has a large chancel, central tower with N and S chapels and nave with aisles. The exterior is imposing but plain; inside, it is full of interesting detail. The flowing window tracery throughout the church is probably the best in Sussex. In the chancel is a set of stalls, nine each side, with carved misericords of various designs, two being of the fox preaching to a congregation of geese. There are elaborate ogee-headed sedilia and piscina. In the chancel floor are two graveslabs with important brasses; one commemorates the founder of the church, Sir William de Etchingham (d.1389), in armour and with inscriptions in Latin and French, and the other shows another Sir William (d.1412), his wife and son (d.1444) under canopies. There are remains too of the original stained glass: armorial glass with the arms of Edward III, the Black Prince and many noble families including the founder's and, in the E window of the N aisle, angels and the symbols of the Evangelists. Among

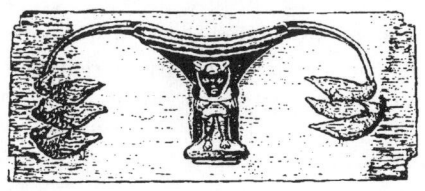

Misericord

the original fittings of the church is the weathervane, the oldest in Sussex, a fret of the Etchingham arms.

Ewhurst *St James* 72E

Ewhurst is on a ridge overlooking Bodiam Castle and the river Rother. The church is noticeable for its shingled spire; the top half is less steep than the base which gives it a twisted appearance from some directions. The lower part of the tower, of the late 12th century, has a round-headed W doorway with a pointed arch above. In the 14th century the aisles were rebuilt (the S aisle retaining the narrow width of the original Norman one), the roof raised, clerestory windows inserted on the S side and a stair turret and upper stage added to the tower; the chancel too is of this date. Inside, the Transitional S arcade has square pillars and square abaci under plain round arches. The 14th-century N arcade has octagonal pillars and pointed arches; the E respond is part of the 12th-century church while the W arch is supported by a corbel of a large face within folded arms. Beneath the corbel is a wall mounted brass of 1520. The 13th-century font is a square bowl of Sussex marble with tapering sides. In the churchyard an 18th-century gravestone near the tower has an uncommon carving of The Resurrection.

Shingled spire

Felpham *St Mary* 99W

'Away to sweet Felpham, for heaven is there' wrote William Blake who, for a few years, lived near the 12th-century church. St Mary's grew during the medieval period. A Norman nave was given a N aisle c.1200 and a S aisle in the 13th century. The W tower dates from the 15th century. Much of the exterior is a mixture of flint and weathered sandstone. Inside, the Transitional N arcade of three bays has circular pillars, large square abaci and arches barely pointed. The capitals have foliage at the corners; the arches have roll moulding above ending in small, worn, animal carvings. The S arcade is typical of the 13th century. Unusual is the contemporary clerestory with trefoil lancets above the N arcade only. The chancel arch is 14th-century; the chancel is of similar age but much restored in the 19th century. The large Norman font is square with shallow arcading. Above the N arcade are the Royal Arms of James I. A marble tablet in the chancel, inscribed with a long poem, commemorates William Hayley, poet and friend of William Blake.

Norman font

Fernhurst *St Margaret of Antioch* 82W

Fernhurst is in the NW of the county close to Blackdown, the highest point in Sussex; the church is just off the village green at the western end. It was built in the 12th century and, although extensively restored in the 19th century, still has original fabric and features. All the modern parts of the church are built in sandstone ashlar; the ancient walls are of plastered stone rubble. Dating from the 12th century are the N and S walls of the chancel and, except for the western end, the nave N wall which has a shallow Norman buttress. To the west of this is a small Norman window, similar to one in the chancel. The S aisle, vestry and tower are entirely modern. In the nave and chancel are ancient tie-beams; set into the N wall of the chancel is a piece of carved masonry, found locally, which may have been a medieval stoup. The large 12th-century cylindrical font has roll moulding and a recessed band halfway down. A 20th-century addition to the church is a set of tapestry kneelers, in co-ordinated colours and designs, depicting the flora and fauna of the area.

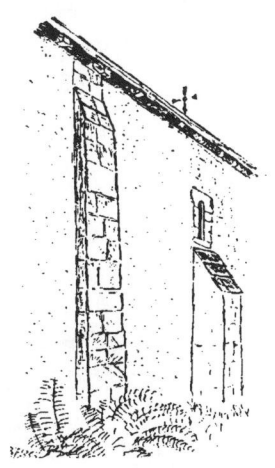

Norman buttress

Ferring *St Andrew*

Old buildings and flint walls identify the former village of Ferring among the modern houses that now surround it. The flint church stands on a mound and, apart from the chancel, is rendered with pebbledash; the small bell turret is tile hung. Extensive alterations occurred in the 13th century and, except for the Norman walls, the present building is mainly Early English. Features of this period are the trefoil-headed windows in the nave S wall, the fine four-bay arcade with round pillars and double-chamfered arches, a holy water stoup in the N aisle inset in a large buttress and the piscina and deeply splayed lancets in the chancel. The blocked doorway (S) was probably the Bishop's private entrance when in residence at his manor nearby. An interesting and unusual memorial to Thomas Oliver (d.1782) has a border carved with a miscellany of motifs: Corinthian pilasters, Adam swags, roses, a skeleton and an hour glass, all surrounding the inscription in verse.

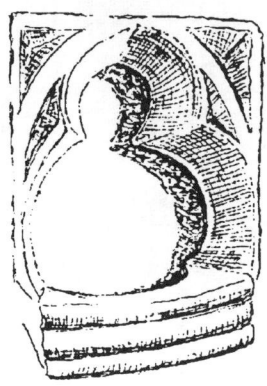
Holy water stoup

Findon *St John*

The main road from Worthing separates Findon village from its church which is reached by a lane to the west. Built of flint with stone dressings, it was extensively restored in the 19th century. The church dates back to the 11th/12th century when it was a cruciform building but this has been changed by later additions; one original arch in the S transept remains. The W tower was added early in the 13th century; it has lancet windows and an arch with a slight chamfer. Later in the same century the chancel arch, vestry and chapel were built. A three-bay Transitional arcade gives onto a N aisle

Sanctus bell opening

which is as wide as the nave itself. Covering both in a single span is a fine timber roof, probably 15th-century; its crown-posts stand on the stonework above the arcade giving the appearance of a twin nave. An old sanctus bell hangs under the roof above the pulpit with a bell-opening in the nave E gable. The 13th-century font, which now has a modern replacement, is at the E end of the aisle. The chapel is entered through an oak screen, a rare survivor from the 13th century.

Firle See **West Firle**.

Fishbourne *St Peter & St Mary* 80W

The church of New Fishbourne, close to the Chichester bypass, is in fields a short distance from the village. Most of the present building, the nave with aisles and bell turret, dates from two major building periods in the 19th century. Surviving from the medieval church is the 13th-century chancel which is separated from the nave by a modern arch of wood. In each side wall are two lancets; there is a piscina (S) and an aumbry (N). The reticulated traceried E window is modern. A fragment of old glass found in the churchyard is set in one of the S lancets; there are two old carved oak benches in the choir. Except for the 1973 extension on the N side of the church, the exterior walls are of flint, part plastered, with stone dressings. Several small crosses cut in the NE quoin of the chancel are thought to have been made by pilgrims travelling from the continent to the shrine of St Richard at Chichester.

Crosses on chancel wall

Fittleworth *St Mary* 01

A painting in the nave shows the church during the restoration of 1870: an Early English tower and chancel with everything between demolished. A Victorian nave, aisles and roof with dormer windows were constructed to fill the gap. A 17th-century N porch was rebuilt and a S porch added. The sandstone tower with low broach spire probably dates from about 1200. It has a peal of six bells, the oldest of 1350. In the S wall is a recess, said to be a seat for bellringers. The chancel has fine simple lancet windows in deep splays. The E window consists of three such lancets; in the N wall are three more, the westernmost with lower sill. Similar windows in the S wall were re-used in the 19th-century vestry. In the nave are the painted Royal Arms of George III. The font, probably 14th-century, has an octagonal bowl decorated with rosettes. In the S porch is an old graveslab with a raised cross; an ancient cross can also be seen in the vestry S gable.

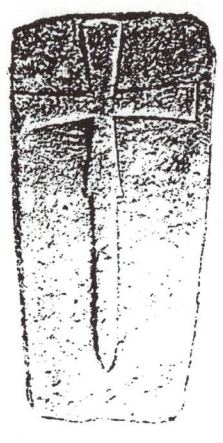
Old graveslab

Fletching *St Andrew & St Mary the Virgin* 42

The large cruciform church at Fletching stands on a Wealden ridge, its shingled broach spire a landmark in the surrounding countryside. The oldest part is the early Norman tower of Tilgate sandstone. Two Norman windows remain in the nave, otherwise the nave, aisles and transepts date from the 13th century. Three of the lancet windows in the transepts contain 14th-century glass found in the churchyard. The long chancel was built during the 19th-century restoration. Both the rood screen and the oak S door with tracery are Perpendicular. Hanging in the nave are funeral achievements of the Neville family, once Lords of the Manor. Memorials in the S transept include a fine early brass (14th-century) of a knight and his lady under a double canopy. A small brass is to a glover who, with other Fletching men, took part in Jack Cade's rebellion. An Elizabethan tomb chest has alabaster effigies of Richard Leche and his wife; a

Memorial brass (detail)

skull between them symbolises the death of a child. The inscription informs us that the widow had the monument made 'of her own accord and herselfe livinge to be pictured lyinge by him'.

Folkington St Peter   50

A narrow lane towards the Downs near Polegate ends at the remote hamlet of Folkington. Its small flint church was built in the 13th century; several Early English lancets remain in the nave and chancel. The (blocked) N doorway was a later addition in the same century. Two Perpendicular windows were inserted in the nave (N wall) c.1400 and the small bell turret was added; the bell itself is of this date. The interior is light and simple with no division between the aisleless nave and chancel. Some old box pews have been retained in the nave which has a roof with tie-beams and crown-posts. In the chancel S wall is a 13th-century piscina. Memorials of the 18th century include a cartouche on the N wall and a wall tablet opposite. Set in the floor in front of the communion rail are several 17th-century ledger slabs. The Perpendicular stone font is octagonal, the stem decorated with pointed trefoil arches. Near the entrance is a carving of Christ by the Sussex sculptor John Skelton.

Ledger slab

Ford St Andrew 90W

From the raised bank of the river Arun, a mile or two inland from the sea, are wide views over the coastal plain with the towers and spires of several churches visible. Ford church is one of these, set in the middle of a field some distance from scattered farms and cottages. It consists of a nave and chancel, a small white bell turret (a landmark for shipping on the river), and a 17th-century brick porch with a Dutch gable. The oldest part is the nave N wall with two small round-headed windows of the 11th century and two larger Norman windows of the

Dutch gable

12th century. The S wall was built in the 15th century after fire had destroyed the S aisle and nave roof. Possibly the finest feature is the plain Norman chancel arch with star decoration around the imposts. The chancel is mainly Norman with Norman and Early English windows in the N and S walls. It was extended in 1320 when the present E window was installed, a good example of reticulated tracery. There is much more of interest in the church: a square font, possibly Saxon, with cover and lock, traces of wall paintings of several periods and a 15th-century roof. Lighting is by candles.

Framfield *St Thomas Becket*

The village is on a Wealden ridge near Uckfield, high enough to give extensive views of the South Downs. Remains of the old church, all but destroyed by fire in 1509, are the 13th-century N chapel and the stair to a rood loft. The church was largely rebuilt in Tudor times when the iron industry made Framfield prosperous; the nave with aisles, clerestory and SE chapel are all in the late Perpendicular style. In 1667 the tower collapsed, the present one dating from 1892. The chancel, too, is 19th-century. Inside are N and S arcades constructed of a local sandstone veined with the rusty colours of iron. The nave has a boarded roof studded with bosses decorated with painted crosses.

17th century clerestory

Ledger slabs pave the central aisle. The S chapel is bright with clear glass windows, some quarries being pre-Reformation glass with a greenish tinge. It contains memorials of the 16th to 18th centuries, one a wall brass of 1595 showing the founder of the chapel and his family. The long squint to the chancel is possibly part of the old church.

Friston *St Mary the Virgin*

Friston is a scattered Downland community a mile inland from the Seven Sisters. The small church originally had a pre-Conquest nave; a blocked window and doorway in the S wall are probably Saxon. In the 12th century the nave was extended westwards and from this period remain round-headed Norman doorways (S porch and N vestry). At the W end is a tile-hung bell turret. A notable interior feature is the 15th-century nave roof with crown-posts, moulded tie-beams and heavy moulded wall plates. The 14th-century chancel has an aumbry, a piscina and a reredos recess in the E wall. Several memorials are to the Selwyns of Friston Place, the earliest a brass of c.1540. A 19th-century N chapel accommodates two large memorials; one in alabaster to Sir Thomas (d.1613) has figures kneeling at a prayer desk with babes in swaddling clothes underneath and six daughters below. From the churchyard, entered by a tapsell gate near the village pond, are views across rolling Downs to Beachy Head and the sea, a reminder of which is a grave with a wooden cross inscribed simply 'Washed Ashore'.

Tapsell gate

Funtington *St Andrew*

The church at Funtington, near Chichester, stands south of the village at the end of a lane. Extensive reconstruction in 1859 left a mainly Victorian exterior and relatively few medieval features. St Andrew's is a large church consisting of chancel with chapels, nave with aisles, W tower, S porch and N vestry. The three-stage tower dates from the 15th century and has diagonal buttresses, square

13th-century arcade

headed openings and a battlemented top. The W window is of three lights with cinquefoil heads under a pointed arch. Surviving from the 13th century are the N chapel and the four bay N arcade (the S arcade is a modern copy). The S chapel is probably 14th-century but both arcades to the chancel and the chancel itself are modern. On the wall of the N chapel is a memorial to a former minister, a cartouche dated 1706. In the tower an 18th-century board records Parish Benefactions from 1658. An unusual wooden memorial of 1671 to Richard Smyth has a coat of arms and inscription. Set in the porch walls are panels from a 15th-century tomb chest.

Glynde St Mary

The medieval church at Glynde, near Lewes, was replaced in 1763-5 by the present classical building, a style rare in a village parish church and unique in Sussex. It was built by Bishop Trevor of Durham who owned the adjoining Elizabethan house, Glynde Place. Rectangular in plan, it is of flint (knapped and squared on the W wall) on a deep ashlar base. Above the projecting W porch is a large stone pediment carrying the Trevor arms surmounted by a bellcote. The interior is an aisleless nave and short chancel, the nave with a W gallery and box pews. All side windows are round-headed; the Venetian E window is framed by coffered rosettes. The blue coved ceiling has white plaster decoration. Several 17th-century ledger slabs from the former church, some with 19th-century brass memorial plates added, are incorporated in the floor; two hatchments are displayed on the nave walls. Small panels and roundels in the chancel windows are 17th-century Flemish glass depicting biblical scenes; the Victorian glass is by Kempe. The marble font, a carved bowl and shaft, dates from the 18th century. A gravestone in the churchyard has a Harmer terracotta (basket of flowers).

Glynde church

Graffham *St Giles* 91W

The church was almost completely rebuilt by G.E.Street in the 1870s as a memorial to Samuel Wilberforce, Bishop of Winchester, who was also Lord of the Manor of Graffham. It consists of chancel with N vestry and S chapel, nave with three-bay arcades to aisles and a W tower with shingled spire. All that remains of the 12th-century Norman church are the two W arches of the arcades, the W pillars and responds. The round pillars are short and have large square scalloped capitals; the arches are of a single order. Of early Norman date is the plain tub-shaped font, similar in pattern and material to several others in W Sussex (e.g. Didling, Selham, Woolbeding). North of the chancel is the doorway to the vestry, re-set from the earlier church; it retains its 15th-century woodwork of vertical oak planks and parts of a lock with, on a complicated catch, the heads of a king and a lady with horned headdress. An ancient part of the exterior is the W doorway from the original 13th-century tower, with nook shafts and moulded capitals and bases.

Vestry doorway

Greatham 01

Greatham church, small and unrestored, stands on a low ridge near the Arun watermeadows between Amberley and Pulborough. It is a single room with ironstone rubble walls in which other materials including flint, chalk and Roman bricks are incorporated. The quoins are roughly shaped blocks of Pulborough sandstone and on three of them are simple incised patterns, possibly consecration crosses. The church was built between the 11th/early 12th centuries, the period of the Saxo-Norman overlap. There is an original window (blocked) in the centre of the E wall and in the N wall are jamb stones of a former

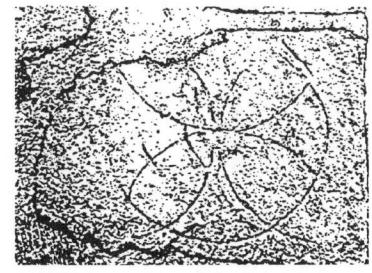

Incised cross

doorway. The lancet windows are 13th-century insertions. At the W end is a bell turret with a small spire. On the floor of the modern porch is a large slab of Sussex marble, possibly a former altar table. The simple interior has whitewashed walls and a crown-post roof; in the E wall are two deeply splayed lancets. The pews and double-decker pulpit date from the early 19th century and there is a 17th-century communion rail. Lighting is by oil lamps.

Guestling *St Laurence* 81E

The church stands with a neighbouring farm in countryside near Hastings. Built of local sandstone and ironstone, it dates from the 11th century and originally consisted of just aisleless nave and chancel. The tower was added c.1100, probably for defence since there was no external access — the present entrance is modern. It has Norman windows and twin bell-openings with baluster shafts. A clasping turret (NW) contains a newel stairway. The chancel, rebuilt in the 13th century, has contemporary clasping buttresses at the eastern corners. Most of the church's interior stonework was renewed after a fire in 1890. In the nave are two-bay arcades to aisles. At the E end of the N aisle is the late 12th-century chapel; the fine entrance has responds with stiff-leaf capitals and an arch with deeply cut chevron ornament. There are lancet windows and round arches to the chancel. The late 13th-century S chapel has a piscina and a squint to the chancel. A monument to John Cheyney (d.1603) and his wife has facing effigies kneeling at a prayer desk.

Norman belfry

Hailsham *St Mary* 50

An earlier church at Hailsham dated from c.1200 and part of the N wall is possibly from this building. The present Perpendicular church of 1425-50 has a battlemented W tower of sandstone blocks alternating with squares of knapped flints; there are two-light bell-openings and corner pinnacles, each with a weathervane. In the 19th century there was considerable rebuilding and the S aisle, porch, vestry and S chapel date from this time. The nave has arcading typical of the Perpendicular style; the clerestory windows above are modern. There are ancient moulded tie-beams in the timber roof. The double sedilia in the chancel is recessed in the S wall; adjoining it is a piscina, one of three in the church. On a chest tomb in the churchyard are the remains of Harmer terracotta urns.

Tower pinnacles

Hamsey St Peter 41

The parish of Hamsey is served by two churches; a modern church at Offham was built to replace the ancient but inconveniently situated church at Hamsey which fortunately escaped demolition. St Peter's, now without a village, stands isolated on rising ground in the Ouse valley. It dates from the early 12th century and has a Norman nave and chancel. The late 14th-century Perpendicular W tower is of generous proportions with a large three-light W window and gargoyles below the battlemented top. The 16th-century porch leads to an unrestored interior with an ancient crown-post roof and few modern fittings. There is a plain Norman arch between nave and chancel. The chancel was extended in the 14th century; the traceried E window dates from c.1350. A canopied tomb chest, carved with shields and quatrefoils, is a memorial to Edward Markwick (d.1538). In the S wall is a piscina, one of three in the church. A blocked 13th-century arch in the nave (N wall) was presumably to a former chapel. Hanging on the walls are funeral hatchments and the Royal Arms of George III. There are old narrow benches and, in a S window, fragments of medieval glass. The 15th-century limestone font is octagonal and carved with cusped arches.

Canopied tomb chest

Hangleton *St Helen* 20

Before Hangleton expanded in the 1950s, St Helen's, now surrounded by modern housing, was a remote Downland church. A simple building of flint with stone dressings, it has an 11th-century nave, a 13th-century tower (with modern battlements and cap) and a chancel of c.1300. A 19th-century restoration fortunately conserved the church's ancient character. The nave, built soon after the Norman Conquest, has herringbone masonry in the S wall confirming its early date. Other Norman details are two small N and S windows, the S doorway and, inside, the N doorway leading to the modern porch and vestry. In the SE corner is a 14th-century ogee-headed piscina. Medieval paintings on the N wall discovered in 1951 have been identified as dating from three periods; the earliest (13th-century) is a band of scroll work about 1.5 m from the ground similar to that in the Norman window splay. Contemporary with the chancel are its trefoil-headed windows; the E window is modern. It is not known who is commemorated by the 16th-century monument (S wall) which has small kneeling figures of parents and children.

Chancel wall

Hardham *St Botolph* 01

Hardham was the first station on the Roman road from Chichester to London and there is Roman material in the fabric of this small early Norman church. It has an 11th-century nave and chancel (the exterior plastered and whitewashed) and a Victorian N porch and bell turret. Three original windows can be seen high up in the walls; the rest were inserted in the 13th and 14th centuries. Inside, too, the walls are plastered. They carry the extensive remains of paintings dating from c.1100. Depicted in the nave are scenes of the Nativity and the parable of Dives and Lazarus, in the chancel scenes of the Passion and Resurrection. The W wall of the chancel shows Adam and Eve, their representation unusual and dramatic. This set of church mural paintings, uncovered in 1866, is one of the most important in the country. One reason for their survival is that they are true frescoes, painted onto the wet plaster which bonded the pigments to the wall. Also to be seen are 15th-century bench ends, a communion rail dated 1720 and the squint of a former anchorite's cell. The church has a bell, probably of the early 12th century, that may be the oldest in Sussex.

Adam and Eve

Hartfield St Mary   43

St Mary's churchyard is entered through a lych gate built into an old timbered cottage. The oldest part of the church (13th-century) is the N wall with rough masonry and one blocked lancet. Of 14th-century date is the S aisle with its Decorated windows, the chancel and S chapel. The Perpendicular W tower with angle buttresses has windows of the 15th century and a tall shingled broach spire; on the E wall is the weather mould of a former steeply pitched roof. Inside, the four-bay nave arcade has octagonal pillars and chamfered arches. The E bay connecting chancel with chapel is wider than the others and of a later date. This and the absence of a chancel arch suggest a substantial rebuilding of this part of the church, possibly in the 16th century. Further evidence can be seen in the roof; there is a double tie-beam where the rood loft and chancel arch are thought to have been. The oldest memorial in the church (1640) is in the S chapel, a tablet with classical columns, cherubs and a long Latin inscription. There are many 19th-century black and white marble wall tablets. At the W end of the aisle is the large octagonal Perpendicular font, its bowl carved with flowers, foliage and shields.

Lych gate

Hastings *All Saints*

Apart from modern vestries, the entire building of chancel, nave with aisles, S porch and W tower dates from the early 15th century. Built of local sandstone with panels of flint chequer work, All Saints' stands above the old town on a west facing hill and, because of the sloping site, steps lead up from tower to nave and nave to chancel. Entrance is through the W door into the tower. This is stone vaulted, the ribs springing from corbels with grotesque heads; a circular opening for the bell ropes is carved with animals. The nave is of four bays with octagonal pillars and capitals; above the chancel arch is a 15th-century Doom painting with Christ seated on two rainbows. Within the E buttress of the S aisle can be seen the rood loft stairs. The chancel has a piscina and triple sedilia with four-centred arches under a flat hoodmould. Memorials in the church include a marble slab with incised effigies of a man and wife (15th-century) and a brass (16th-century). On the walls are the painted Royal Arms of George II and six funeral hatchments. The 15th-century octagonal font is decorated with arches, quatrefoils and shields. Under the tower are 18th-century text boards and verses about the pleasures and penalties of bellringing.

Bellringers' board

Hastings *St Clement*

When the French raided Hastings in 1377 they burnt the town including St Clement's church. The present Perpendicular church was built shortly afterwards and, except for a modern S porch and a 15th-century sanctuary, is entirely of the late 14th century. The SW battlemented tower, of chequered flint and stone, has large three and four-light windows and, inside, a vaulted roof with decorative leaf carvings. Seven-bay arcades to N and S aisles have pillars with shafts and hollow mouldings. There is no structural division between nave and chancel, though niches are set into the pillars at this point; an ancient screen once stood across the church here and fragments of it are displayed at the W end. The fine octagonal font is early 15th-century and has shields carved with the instruments of the Passion, including the cross and crown of thorns. Two handsome brass chandeliers in the nave were donated in the 18th century. Among the many memorials is a large, imposing wall tablet in the chancel to John Collier, d.1760. On the E wall of the S aisle are two panels of Moses and Aaron painted by Roger Mortimer. He may also have painted the decorated Benefaction board on the W wall of the tower, dated 1721.

Statuary niche

Heathfield *All Saints* 52

All Saints' is situated at Old Heathfield in an extensive parish containing several other communities of the High Weald; the present church of Hastings sandstone was built to accommodate a large congregation. It consists of a W tower with shingled broach spire, a wide lofty nave with clerestory, four-bay arcades to N and S aisles and a chancel (all of the 13/14th centuries). The N and S porches and SE chapel date from the 19th-century restoration. The windows show details of the Decorated style; the W window is of triple lancets with cusped trefoil heads, the clerestory lights are quatrefoils and the E window an elaboration of intersecting tracery. The aisle is paved with 18th-century ledger slabs. Four hatchments hang in the nave and above the tower arch are the Royal Arms of George III. Among the churchyard memorials are some by Jonathan Harmer who worked as mason and potter in Heathfield in the early 19th century. He produced gravestones decorated with terracotta plaques and ornament which can be found in Sussex churchyards. Some of the original moulds are in the Barbican Museum at Lewes.

Harmer plaque

Hellingly *St Peter & St Paul*

Circular churchyards may be an indication of Saxon age and occur at a few places in Sussex, such as Hellingly. There is Norman work in parts of the walls and two small round-headed windows in the chancel. Inside, these windows have deep splays and shafts of late 12th-century design with bobbin-ring moulding and foliage capitals; the palm leaf frieze beneath is also of this date. The rest of the chancel windows are narrow lancets of the 13th century. Later in this century the N transept was built; the E wall has arcading with shafts around lancet windows (elaborate for a village church) and a N window has intersecting tracery. The nave aisle arcades are typical of the 14th century. The W tower was built in the 19th century; its wide arch contains a screen, gallery and organ. On the chancel floor is a brass to a lady (c.1440) with good details of robe and horned headdress. The remains of a carved Norman font are set in the chapel W wall. There are three Harmer terracottas in the churchyard.

Palmette frieze

Henfield *St Peter*

Churchyard yews

St Peter's stands on the highest point of Henfield a short distance from the village street. The attractive churchyard has paths lined with over a hundred clipped yews. Records show that by 1250 there was a small church of Caen stone; this was enlarged in the 14th and 15th centuries and then stayed almost unaltered until extensive restoration in Victorian times. Entrance is through the 15th-century tower; the porch occupies the ground floor and a low S door gives access to the chambers above.

The church has a ring of eight bells. Of the original building remain the nave walls, two lancet windows (now in the S vestry) and the wide chancel arch. The chancel itself was completely rebuilt during the restoration. Four-bay arcades (late 13th-century) give onto N and S aisles which have modern transepts. North of the chancel is the 15th-century Parham chapel, built in the Perpendicular style with a splendid five-light window and an E window which, although quite different, is contemporary. The wooden screen door is also 15th-century. Nearly 300 modern tapestry kneelers, each with a different design, depict the flora and fauna of the Parish.

Herstmonceux *All Saints* 61

Herstmonceux is best known for its 15th-century brick castle. Nearby is the church which predates it by several centuries. The NW tower, built of sandstone in the late 12th century, has uncommon triple lancet-shaped bell-openings and a later shingled broach spire. Of similar age is the two-bay N arcade with foliage capitals and pointed arches. The rest of the nave, N and S aisles, S porch and chancel are 13th and 14th-century. About 1440, contemporary with the castle, the N chapel was built of brick and the E chancel wall rebuilt similarly. The dormer windows are a Victorian addition. The 14th-century square font stands on a circular central shaft with four supporting octagonal columns. In the chancel aisle is a large brass of a knight in armour under a canopy and with a Norman French inscription commemorating Sir William Fiennes who died in 1402. Between the chancel and N chapel is the grandiose monument to Thomas, Lord Dacre (d.1533) and his son (d.1528). It consists of a tomb chest with decorated panels and two recumbent effigies, the whole covered by a vaulted canopy rising as high as the top of the walls. A 19th-century marble tablet (chancel N wall) depicts a bedside scene with mourning figures. In the churchyard are several Harmer terracotta plaques.

The Dacre tomb

Heyshott *St James* 81W

The original Early English church at Heyshott consisted of chancel, nave and narrow N aisle; in the 19th century the chancel was rebuilt, the aisle widened and the vestry and porch were added. Remaining from the 13th-century church are the S and W nave walls and, inside, the three-bay nave arcade with pointed double-chamfered arches on circular pillars and abaci. Nave windows (S and W) of two trefoil-headed lights with a sexfoil above are probably late 14th-century. In one N aisle window are small pieces of old glass depicting angels playing musical instruments. The glass was removed during the Victorian restoration, passing through several hands before being returned to the church in 1912. All the fittings are modern except for the font which may date from the 13th century and appears to have been altered from its original form. It is tub-shaped with roll moulding round the rim and has four small shafts with capitals carved into it at the bottom; the oak cover is 17th-century. Preserved nearby is a fragment of a pillar piscina. The painted Royal Arms (18th-century) hang above the S door.

14th-century window

Hollington *St Leonard* 71E

Situated on the western outskirts of Hastings, St Leonard's is known locally as 'The Church in the Wood'. Though still peacefully sheltered by trees, today modern housing development lies immediately beyond. St Leonard's is largely the result of a major reconstruction in 1865. The little that remains of a 13th-century church includes part of the W wall, the nave N wall and the N doorway now leading to a modern vestry. In

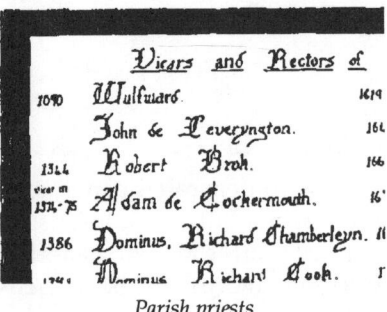
Parish priests

the nave wall is an ancient piscina, possibly reset; there is one old tie-beam in the roof. A board records the names of vicars and rectors of Hollington, starting with Wulfward, 1090. The bell turret houses a 14th-century bell.

Hooe *St Oswald* 60

Hooe church is at the end of a narrow lane some distance from the village. It was largely rebuilt in the 15th century and from this period are the tower, the nave, chancel and S porch. Some windows have heads as label stops. An earlier part is the 13th-century N chapel (now used as a vestry) with tall narrow lancets in the N and W walls; the E end is a later brick replacement. Large leaves are carved in the spandrels of the S entrance and corbels on each side of the porch carry stone seats. Corbels in the nave walls and two blocked doorways (SE) remain from a former rood loft. In the N wall are three 15th-century windows and a recess formed by the blocked N door. The 12th-century square font is of Sussex marble and rests on a central stem with four shafts. Reset in the chancel E window are pieces of medieval stained glass with figures of the Coronation of the Virgin. The S wall has a sedile and piscina. Old woodwork in the church includes the 17th-century communion rail, the hexagonal sounding board with inlay of c.1700 (the pulpit is modern) and an ancient oak dugout chest.

Label stop

Horsham *St Mary* ✓ 13

Horsham has one of the largest parish churches in Sussex; it stands near the river Arun and is built of local stone. Of an earlier Norman church remain a round-headed doorway and a narrow window (N wall) and the lower part of the tower. The present building dates from the 13th century. The tower, with massive buttresses, is finished with a

East window

corbel table and a tall shingled spire. In 1307 the N chantry chapel was added; the sacristy and S chapel are 15th-century and the gabled S aisle extension dates from 1865. Inside, the nave has five-bay arcades and a clerestory, notable Early English work. Wall shafts each side to clerestory level mark the division between nave and chancel. The impressive seven-light E window is a replica of the former Perpendicular design; the glass is 19th-century as in all other windows. The canopied Purbeck marble tomb of Thomas Hoo (d.1485) has carved pendants, fan vaulting and an angel playing a lute. An effigy of a knight in armour commemorates Thomas, Lord Braose (d.1395). A marble monument to Elizabeth Delves (d.1654) has a life sized recumbent figure on a classical tomb. There are 18th-century memorials under the tower and two funeral hatchments on the W wall. The Perpendicular octagonal font is carved with a Tudor rose design.

Horsted Keynes *St Giles* 32

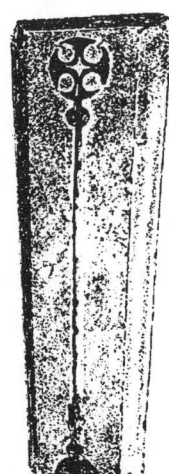
Tapered graveslab

St Giles' is in a dip below the village but its tall sharply pointed spire is visible for miles above the trees of the Weald. Originally it was a Norman cruciform church of which the lower tower and possibly the lower walls of nave and chancel remain. In the 13th century the S transept, nave and chancel were rebuilt, all with narrow lancet windows; the Norman N transept has gone. The N chapel dates from the 14th century. A N aisle, added in the Victorian restoration, has a small reset Norman doorway. A blocked arch in the chancel S wall shows that formerly a S chapel existed. The oldest part within the church is the tower crossing, three plain Norman arches on slightly chamfered square imposts; the pointed W arch is 14th-century. The plain octagonal font is of the 15th century. In the chancel N wall is a small tomb recess with trefoil head containing a tiny effigy of a cross-legged knight. Near it is a tapering marble graveslab with a raised cross. The churchyard contains gravestones of 17th and 18th centuries. Two huge 17th-century ledger slabs, originally in the S chapel, are set on the outside wall of the chancel.

Houghton *St Nicholas* 01

Although largely rebuilt in the 19th century, the small flint church at Houghton keeps its Early English character and simplicity. Situated on the N slope of the Arun gap it consists of a chancel, nave with W bellcote and S porch. All the windows are lancets, single on the north and south, of two lights with a circular opening above in the W wall and in the E wall a group of three with narrow stonework between. The nave, unaisled and spacious, is separated from the chancel by a pointed arch (modern). On either side and on the chancel E wall are creed, prayer and commandment boards. The 19th-century pulpit and pews are of pine as is the timber roof. At the W end stands the huge octagonal font, probably dating from the 15th century, supported on a stem of similar shape and proportions. On the floor nearby are large slabs of Sussex marble, one with a small brass inscribed in Latin to Thomas Cheyne (d.1496). There are several 18th-century gravestones in the churchyard, one (NW) with a Resurrection carving.

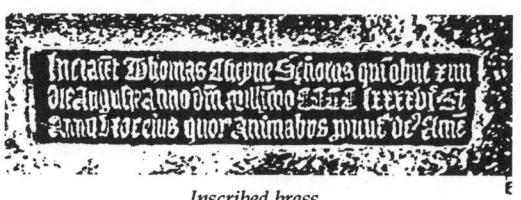
Inscribed brass

Icklesham *All Saints* 81E

This impressive large church is basically early Norman, modified in the late 12th and 13th/14th centuries. It has a nave with aisles and a chancel longer than the nave. North of the chancel is the tower and a chapel, to the south the large chapel of St Nicholas. The oldest parts are Norman: the tower of three stages with shallow buttresses, the N doorway and various window openings. In the fine Norman nave are three-bay arcades with semicircular arches of two orders on massive round pillars and capitals decorated with scallops and foliage. The S

Blind arcade

aisle still has its small 12th-century windows, the N aisle has 14th-century insertions. At the end of both aisles are early Norman arches. The northern one opens into the tower which has a stone vaulted roof added c.1200. The chancel was extended in the 13th/14th centuries when the S chapel was built; both have windows in the Decorated style. The chancel E window is the result of 19th-century restoration. The chapels have blind arcades with 12th-century carved shafts, thought to have been taken from the chancel and re-used during the medieval rebuilding.

Iden *All Saints* 92E

The church dates from the early 12th century but the original building has been considerably enlarged; nave aisles were added (the S aisle was later demolished) and in the 13th century the chancel was rebuilt. In the early 15th century the N chapel was added and the N aisle widened. Though mainly rebuilt, the tower retains a Norman N wall with one window. Carved on the label stops of the W doorway are angels holding shields. Inside the nave can be seen the blocked arches of the former S arcade; the square central pier has a stoup in its N face. The two-bay N arcade has pointed arches and an octagonal pillar; two 15th-century windows in the aisle have cinquefoil lights. The high tower arch is of three moulded orders; the chancel arch dates from c.1420. In the chancel S wall is a 14th-century piscina; a blocked priest's doorway is visible outside. A brass on the N wall with a figure in Mass vestments is to Walter Seller (d.1427), a former rector. The 15th-century limestone font is octagonal in bowl, stem and base.

Blocked arcade

Ifield *St Margaret*

Ifield church is on the western edge of Crawley with town housing on one side, open fields on the other. The exterior is roughcast with stone dressings. The chancel is early 13th-century with some lancet windows. The spacious nave has arcades of the early 14th century with octagonal pillars and double-chamfered arches. In the clerestory are seen two window styles: 14th-century cusped trefoils and flat-headed Perpendicular lights. Above is a wide medieval roof with tie-beams and crown-posts. The wooden N porch dates from the 15th century. During the restoration of 1883 the nave was extended and the W tower with shingled broach spire was built. The 12th-century font of Sussex marble has a typical Norman form, a square bowl on a central column with four supporting shafts; uncommon however is the decoration, roll mouldings and waterleaf foliage. Beneath the E arches of the nave are two tomb chests with recumbent effigies, thought to be Sir John de Ifelde (d.1340) and his wife Margaret (d.1347). The carvings are of high quality with angels at the head, lions at the feet and good details of costume and accoutrements. In the tower are the painted Royal Arms of George II and a carved monogram of Charles II.

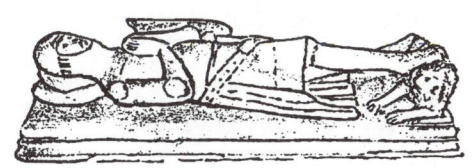

Stone effigy

Iford *St Nicholas*

Iford overlooks the Ouse watermeadows two miles south of Lewes. Its early 12th-century Norman church, of flint with sandstone dressings, originally consisted of nave and chancel only. Later in the same century a tower was constructed above the chancel space and the present chancel was built to the east. Access to this is through two arches in the massive walls of the tower; the one facing the nave (the original chancel arch) has a roll moulding decoration with intermittent chevrons. In the E wall of the

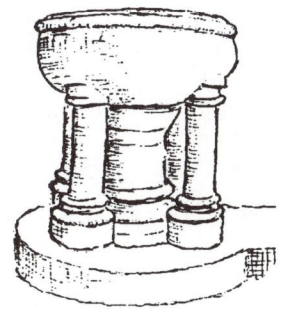

13th-century font

chancel are three narrow round-headed windows, deeply splayed, with an oculus above; these were uncovered during the 19th-century restoration. A blocked Transitional arcade in the nave once opened onto a 12th-century N aisle which was demolished about a century later. The S doorway and porch are modern. The church possesses three bells of the 15th century and a fine Early English font, bowl-shaped on a circular column and four supporting shafts.

Isfield *St Margaret* 41

A shift in population has left Isfield church in peaceful isolation by the river Ouse. In a reconstruction of the nave in 1876 the N aisle was added to the medieval building; the S wall survives from the 13th century. The W tower was probably rebuilt in the 15th century and now has a Victorian top and spire. Inside is the church's oldest feature, the late 12th-century tower arch, pointed and with a slight chamfer. Both chancel and S chapel, with a squint between, are from the Decorated period. The chancel has a fine traceried E window; in the S wall are sedilia and a large piscina under a gable with crocketed shafts. A lancet window in the nave (S) contains 14th-century glass. The linenfold panelling and benches with poppy heads date from the 16th century when the Shurley family adopted the chapel. It houses their monuments, the earliest of which is to Sir John (d.1527), a tombchest with shields. There are brasses to Edward (d.1558) and his wife and Thomas (d.1579) and his wife. The large alabaster monument has recumbent effigies of Sir John (d.1631) and his two wives with nine kneeling children below.

Piscina

Itchingfield *St Nicholas* 12

Itchingfield church, SW of Horsham, belonged to Sele Priory until the Dissolution of the monasteries. In the churchyard is the tiny priest's house thought to have been used by visiting monks. It is timber-framed infilled with lath and plaster and brick nogging, parts of it dating from the 15th century. The church itself (nave and chancel) was built in the early 12th century and of this remain the N and W walls, several round-headed windows and the original W doorway. The doorway now leads into the 15th-century W tower or belfry, unique in Sussex being built completely of wood. Four massive oak beams, 50 cm square, support the structure, thick planks form the walls and above is now a 19th-century shingled broach spire. The Victorian S aisle contains a reset 15th-century window. All roofs are of Horsham slabs. Inside, there is no arch between nave and chancel, a wooden screen from the 15th century providing the division. Above the W door is a Decorated window, pre-dating the tower. Built into the chancel N wall is a round-headed Norman aumbry discovered during the 19th-century restoration.

Priest's house

Jevington *St Andrew*   50

The village of Jevington lies along a Downland coomb near Eastbourne; it was inhabited in pre-Conquest times when its original flint church was built. The large, low tower is from this period, the recognisable Saxon features being the long and short work (NE quoins) and the blocked N and S windows with arches of Roman bricks. The belfry openings have original baluster shafts, re-used in the 19th-century restoration. In the 13th century a N aisle was added; its lancet windows are typical of the Early English period as is the narrow chancel arch. There is an aumbry (14th-century) in the N wall of the chancel and in the S wall a trefoil-headed shelved piscina. In the nave are Perpendicular style windows (c.1500); the wagon roof has alternate hammer beams and crown-posts. A tablet set in the N wall is a rare example of Saxon

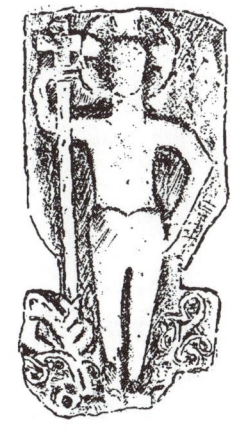

Saxon carving

sculpture, found during repair work in the belfry. The carving in relief is thought to represent the Resurrected Christ holding a long cross-headed staff which is thrust into the mouth of a beast at His feet.

Keymer *St Cosmas & St Damian* 31

A drawing in the Burrell Collection shows Keymer church as it was about 1780: a medieval church comprising a W tower with broach spire, nave with Horsham slab roof and an apsidal chancel. This church was all but demolished in 1866 and rebuilt. Remaining from the old structure are a 15th-century window reset in the N aisle and the rough flintwork of the Norman apse, noteworthy as one of the five ancient apses in Sussex. The rest consists of the Victorian nave with N and S aisles and a SW tower with broach spire. The dedication, one of only three in the country, is to the patron saints of Pharmacy and Medicine, Cosmas and Damian, North African physician brothers who were martyred for their Christian beliefs in the 4th century. They are depicted in a modern ceramic tablet mounted on the N aisle wall.

Norman apse

Kingston *St Pancras* 30

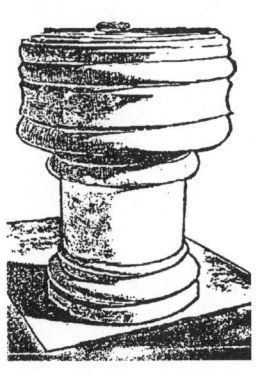
Font

Kingston's village street runs towards the Downs and continues as a footpath to the ridge. A churchyard tapsell gate near the end of the street gives access to the flint church which is almost entirely of the Decorated period. It consists of a nave and chancel (c.1300) and a slender W tower which may be slightly earlier. The S porch is modern; the medieval N doorway now leads into a vestry added in 1960. A two-light window with a quatrefoil under a pointed arch is repeated and arranged symmetrically throughout the nave and chancel. The tower arch springs from the side walls of the tower; a wide chancel arch gives spaciousness and light to the interior as does the large three-light E window. Two narrow windows in the chancel, different from the rest, may have been in an earlier church; externally these are seen to be headed with sandstone blocks roughly carved with ogee arches. A disused priest's doorway (S wall) has an arch of re-used stone with a flint key-stone. The circular font is heavily moulded on bowl and stem. Near it is a fine Jacobean carved chest. The church was restored in the 19th century following severe damage by lightning.

Kingston Buci *St Julian* 20

Remains of anchorite's cell

Kingston gets its second name from Ralph de Buci who held the manor after the Conquest. Foundations of a Saxon church were discovered beneath the nave in 1964 but the present church dates from the late 11th century. In the 13th century the central tower, chancel, N aisle (rebuilt in the 19th century) and S porch were built. The exterior, mainly of flint and stone rubble, shows evidence of changes over the centuries. A small door and a splayed recess in the chancel N wall mark the position of an anchorite's cell. Inside, striking architectural features are the Early English N arcade and the tower with quadripartite vaulting rising from clustered shafts. There are many interesting furnishings: from the 12th century a square sandstone font, from the 15th the chancel screen, the rector's stall and some stained glass fragments. A Renaissance recessed tomb in the chancel has remains of religious carvings. Elizabethan linenfold panelling is incorporated in the two-decker pulpit. The 17th-century singing desk with pitchpipe is thought to be unique. In 1988 the church interior was rearranged, the nave and aisle forming the body of the church with the sanctuary to the south.

Kirdford *St John the Baptist* 02

Kirdford church is built of coarse Bargate stone, a sandy limestone quarried below the W Sussex Downs, and roofed with Horsham slabs.

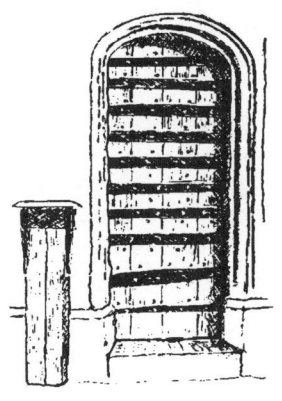

Oak door and poorbox

From the early 12th-century church remain the Norman S doorway (blocked) and part of the nave S wall. The 15th-century W tower, of three stages, has a plain parapet and pyramidal cap. An ancient W porch leads into the tower where an original oak door gives access to a newel stairway; near it stands a poor box. The high arch to the nave is of three chamfered orders. The three-bay N arcade and aisle date from the 13th century. Two original aisle lancets remain, one containing fragments of medieval glass possibly made in local furnaces; at the E end is a Decorated window with reticulated tracery. The chancel was rebuilt in the 14th/15th centuries with a lean-to sacristy on the north; squints on either side of the modern chancel arch date from this period as does the trefoil-headed piscina. Old woodwork includes the fine 17th-century communion rail, the Ringers' Gallery balustrade in the tower and a number of 16th-century benches in the N aisle. The plain octagonal font of Sussex marble, a stone quarried at Kirdford until the 19th century, is inscribed with the date 1620 and the initials of two churchwardens.

Lancing *St James the Less* 10

St James' in North Lancing is situated in a street of old houses and built of flint and roughcast. Preserved from the original 12th-century church is a fine S doorway with shafts, stiff-leaf foliage and deep moulding, reset in a later porch, and part of a string course with billet decoration in the chancel. The font, a shallow square bowl of marble, is Norman. About 1300 the church was almost entirely rebuilt. It has a wide nave with narrow aisles, a central tower, chancel and S porch. The nave arcades have octagonal pillars and double-chamfered arches, as do the four arches under the tower crossing. There

South porch

are windows typical of this period, narrow lancets with trefoil heads; two in the chancel are in the 'low side' position set within arched recesses. Later insertions are the the circular clerestory lights and the Perpendicular windows. In the chancel N wall is a 14th-century tomb recess, now containing a medieval graveslab. During the 17th century the church fell into decay, 'pigeons breeding in the church' and 'the chancel not fit for communion'. After the tower had partly collapsed, its height was reduced and the present pyramidal cap added.

Laughton   All Saints ✓

The original seat of the Pelham family was at Laughton and the village church, like several others in E Sussex, has a 'Pelham tower'. These are Perpendicular towers solidly constructed of ashlar and decorated, in honour of the donors, with the family badge, the Pelham buckle. At Laughton this is seen on the label stops of the W doorway. The aisleless nave, wide and long, dates from the 13th century; there are two lancet windows of this period. The remainder of the nave windows are Perpendicular, as are the tower and chancel arches. The chancel is of the 18th century, an early example of the Gothic Revival. On the exterior, the priest's doorway has an ornate ogee arch and the walls are adorned with crocketed pinnacles. To the north of the chancel is the Pelham vault, built in the 18th century, in which more than thirty members of the family are interred. Medieval niches and a piscina can be seen inside the nave; two helms and the Royal Arms of George III hang on the walls. Carved tracery from an ancient rood screen has been re-used in the panelling behind the altar.

Priest's doorway

Lewes   St Anne ✓

This 12th-century flint church stands above the High Street at the west end of the town. The tower is Norman as are the nave, the S chapel and part of the chancel (the E end is a 13th-century extension). Most of

Norman font

the windows are 19th-century replacements. Inside, a notable architectural feature is the Transitional four-bay S arcade which dates from the late 12th century. It has round pillars, square abaci and capitals with stiff-leaf foliage; carvings beneath are all different. At this time the chapel was given its vaulted roof and the W arch made to connect aisle and chapel. The nave roof of tie-beams and queen-posts was constructed in 1538. On the 18th-century W gallery are the handsome Royal Arms of George IV. A local craftsman carved the oak pulpit in 1620. The fine Norman font, cylindrical in shape, has basketweave decoration between bands of pellet and plait ornament. An anchorite's cell was discovered during the building of the modern vestry; in the chancel S wall is part of the original squint. A large number of iron grave markers can be seen in the churchyard.

Lewes *St John the Baptist*

Gundrada's tombslab

Southover church has many associations with nearby Lewes Priory. The ruins of the gatehouse are built into the churchyard wall, the church itself was originally the Priory guesthouse and the founder, William de Warenne, and his wife Gundrada are buried in the chapel. The present building consists of a nave (14th-century), S aisle (16th-century), W tower (18th-century) and a chancel with S chapel and vestry (19th-century). The battlemented tower is the dominant external feature. Constructed of red brick with a black chequer pattern, it is finished with a 19th-century cupola and tall weathervane in the shape of a shark. The nave N wall contains modern replacements of the original Decorated windows. The S aisle is faced with a chequer pattern of stone and flint and has Tudor three-light windows under four-centred arches. The oldest part of the church is the 12th-century S arcade with four short round pillars and semicircular arches. The nave still has its medieval roof, tie-beams with crown-posts and curved braces. In the Norman-style chapel are the remains and burial caskets of William de Warenne and Gundrada, uncovered during the building of the railway. Set in the floor is the great treasure of the church, the black Tournai marble tombslab of Gundrada.

Lewes *St Michael*

A distinctive feature of St Michael's is the round tower, one of only three in Sussex, the others being at Southease and Piddinghoe. Built of flint, it was once plastered but is now covered with pebbledash. A tall shingled spire, twisted by wind and weather, rises above it. Only the tower and the wall to which it is attached remain from the original 13th-century building. Inside, the three-bay S arcade dates from the 14th century. Following periods of decline and neglect, the church became dilapidated and extensive restoration work was undertaken in 1748. The S aisle was rebuilt and its exterior wall of knapped and squared flints fronts onto the High Street. The N arcade was constructed with wooden pillars designed to match those opposite and these continue through to both sides of the chancel. In the 19th century the chancel was extended and vestries built. Two 15th-century brasses of a knight and a priest are reset on the N wall. A memorial tablet has kneeling figures of Sir Nicholas Pelham (d.1559) and his wife, with smaller figures of their ten children below. The modern sculpture of St Michael, by Harry Phillips, was mounted on the tower in 1976.

View from the castle

Lewes *St Thomas à Becket* 41

This church is believed to have been founded as a chapel of ease in the 12th century by the college of canons at South Malling. The chancel is possibly the original chapel but no obviously Norman work is visible.

The Royal Arms of Elizabeth I

The body of the present church (nave and aisles) is of the 14th century; the windows are in the Perpendicular style. The tower, built in the 15th century, is of knapped flint with random squared blocks of stone. A vestry was added in the 19th century. Entrance to the nave is by the W door and tall tower arch. There are three-bay arcades with small clerestory windows above the spandrels of the arches; those on the S side are blocked, those on the north are covered by dormer windows in the roof. A charity tablet and a copy of a medieval charter are displayed in the tower. In the S aisle are a piscina, stoup and squint. On the W wall are two Royal Arms, the lower of George I; the upper, made of plaster, are the oldest in Sussex (1598). They show the Tudor Arms of Queen Elizabeth supported by the lion of England and the dragon of Wales.

Linch *St Luke* 82W

There is no village of Linch. The medieval parish consisted of a southern part under the Downs near Bepton, where there was a church, and a separate part six miles to the north, where there was a chapel. Both buildings had long been in ruins when in 1700 a new chapel was raised on the site of the old one at Woodman's Green. The nave of St Luke's, built of small squared blocks of local sandstone, is basically this chapel. In the 19th century a chancel, S vestry, organ chamber, spire and

The Ascension

S porch were added. Most of the details (windows and fittings) are Victorian but in a N window are two panels of 15th-century German stained glass depicting the Descent from the Cross and Christ Ascending (note the footprints). Dating from 1700 is the S doorway with four-centred arch and an inscription above: APRIL THE FIRST 1700 PETER BETTESWORTH WAS CHOSE CHVRCH WARDEN FOR TWO REPAIRE AND REBVILD THIS CHAPPEL IN LINCH.

Linchmere *St Peter* 83W

The village is a mile from the Surrey border in the far NW of Sussex. St Peter's is high in the Greensand hills with a superb view to the south, also visible from inside the church through a glass door in the S wall. The nave dates from the 12th century; the W doorway, now leading to a vestry, is tall and round-headed and the small lancet above the pulpit probably originated as a Norman window. The 13th-century chancel has contemporary lancets, a piscina and an E window with plate tracery (two lancets with a circle above). At the W end of the nave are two tall columns and pointed arches which support a 17th-century stone bell turret; on the exterior this is tiled and shingled and resembles a typical Sussex timber-framed turret. The double N aisle and vestry are modern (19th and 20th centuries). Marking the division between nave and chancel is an old moulded tie-beam with baluster and arched braces above. On the N wall is a medieval carving from France of seven monks representing the Seven Deadly Sins.

The Seven Deadly Sins

Lindfield *All Saints*   32

In medieval times Lindfield was an important iron working centre and its large church built in the 13/14th centuries reflects the population

Curvilinear tracery

and prosperity of that period. Built of stone under Horsham slab roofs, it has an aisled nave, chancel with chapels and a W tower with a tall broach spire. Of 14th-century date are the transepts and fine two-storeyed porch with contemporary oak door. On each side of the porch is a mass dial; the parvise above is used as a local museum. Inside, the Decorated nave arcades have octagonal pillars and chamfered arches; the chancel arcades are Perpendicular with slim, moulded pillars and four-centred arches. The Decorated E window of five lights and flowing tracery is similar to that at Etchingham. In the S chapel are two corbels carved with angels holding shields (E wall) and a piscina (S wall). The carved octagonal font dates, unusually, from the time of Henry VIII. The oldest memorial is a brass to Richard Challoner (d.1501); two other brasses date from the 17th century and there are 18th-century wall tablets and ledger slabs. Painted achievements and charity boards are mounted on the nave and tower walls.

Litlington 50

Litlington lies near the river in the Cuckmere valley, a mile south of Alfriston. Its small flint church has a Norman nave and chancel dating from c.1150. The W end, rebuilt in the 14th century, has a low doorway and a weatherboarded bell turret with a shingled spire. Also 14th-century is the porch which has a mass dial, one of three in the church walls (two others are in the NW wall). Original Norman details which survive include the S doorway, two windows in the chancel N wall and, in the nave, a string course. The Perpendicular font of green sandstone has an octagonal bowl, stem and base. At the W end is a stairway to the belfry, lit by small openings. In the nave roof are old tie-beams; the chancel roof has embattled wall plates and

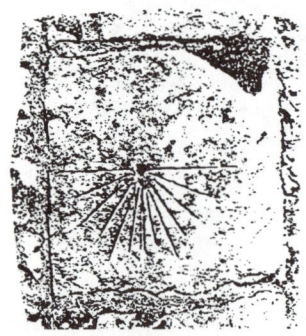
Mass dial

carved wooden corbels and bosses. The Perpendicular tomb in the chancel N wall was used for the Easter Sepulchre. In the S wall are a piscina, double sedilia and a low side window.

Little Horsted *St Michael*   41

This tiny community of a few houses, farms and a church is situated about seven miles NE of Lewes. The oldest part of the church is the Norman chancel; on the exterior N wall is an arcade of four Norman arches of rusty sandstone, two of them containing small round-headed windows. Inside the chancel, almost hidden by choir stalls, is a low tomb recess containing a medieval tapering slab with a raised cross. The nave was built in the 19th century, as was the N porch and the vestry recess off the chancel. At the west end is the fine Perpendicular tower of c.1500 built of green sandstone ashlar. Carved in the spandrels of the W doorway are a Tudor rose and a Green Man. The very high tower arch reaches to the apex of the nave roof.

Green Man

Lodsworth *St Peter*   92W

Lodsworth, a quiet village set in lovely countryside near Midhurst, has a long narrow street lined with attractive cottages. A lane to the southeast leads down to the church and nearby manor house. The only medieval part of the church remaining is the early 14th-century tower, the rest being 19th-century rebuilding mainly in the Gothic style or, as in the S transept, neo-Norman. The unbuttressed tower appears to have some original plaster and is quite unrestored. The weathered W doorway has a pointed arch and jamb

West doorway

shafts with moulded capitals; to the south is a square-headed holy water stoup with a damaged bowl. The second stage houses six bells, three dating from the 17th century; the roof is pyramidal with projecting eaves. The pointed arch to the nave rests on square responds with no imposts. In the nave floor are 18th-century gravestones. There are old tie-beams in the roof; attached to these and to the moulded wall plates are carved wooden bosses of various designs. Mounted on the 18th-century oak vestry screen are the Royal Arms of Queen Victoria.

Lullington 50

The tranquil, secluded place where Lullington church is situated can be reached by crossing the river near Alfriston church and continuing along a footpath for about half a mile. The church is about 5m square and has a white weatherboarded bell turret. Often described as one of the smallest churches in the country, it is actually the chancel of a larger church, remains of which can be seen to the west of the entrance. There are five windows; four are 14th-century and one on the N side dates from the 13th century. Traces of low side windows can be seen and there is a piscina in the sanctuary. The church was restored in 1894.

The church

Lurgashall *St Lawrence* 92W

Lurgashall is under Blackdown, accessible only along narrow lanes. Its focal point is the beautiful village green with the church on one side. The nave N wall is of shaly ironstone rubble with some herringbone work, built no later than the 11th century; on both N and S walls are shallow Norman buttresses. The chancel is Early English and the N chapel modern. The 14th-century S tower had a timber spire until the 1950s when it had to be taken down; a metal structure supports the new spire of 1968. Unique in Sussex is the 16th-century timber lean-to gallery running the length of the nave S wall; originally a village meeting place, it was used subsequently as a school and part of it now forms a porch for the S entrance. The nave interior has high walls and a tall, blocked N doorway, both indicative of Saxon influence. On the S wall are the remains of 14th-century paintings with coats of arms. The font, a huge square block of Sussex marble with rusticated sides, bears the date 1662.

Timber gallery

Among the memorials is a wall tablet of 1728 with fine Baroque ornament. In the chancel are two church chests of the 17th and 18th centuries.

Lyminster *St Mary Magdalene* 00

There was a Benedictine nunnery at Lyminster in Saxon times and St Mary Magdalene was possibly its church, the nuns using the chancel, the parishioners the nave. The Saxon origins of the church are apparent from the tall, narrow proportions of nave and chancel, their thin walls, the chancel arch and the blocked S doorway. Norman features are the blocked S doorway (beneath the Saxon one) and a W entrance, now the tower arch. A N aisle was added in the 12th century; a huge tiled roof covers nave and aisle. The lower part of the tower dates from the 13th century, the upper stage from the 15th. The 15th-century N porch contains original woodwork. There is a variety of windows: blocked Saxon or Norman openings, Early English style lancets, a Perpendicular E window and a round window of uncertain age in the nave S wall. Inside, the dominant features are the lofty nave, the high chancel arch with double imposts and the pillars of the Transitional arcade with scalloped capitals and stiff-leaf decoration. The simple square piscina in the chancel is 12th-century or earlier, the plain font of Sussex marble typically Norman.

Chancel arch

Madehurst *St Mary* 91W

Madehurst is a quiet hamlet in wooded Downland near Arundel. Its church was greatly restored in the 19th century though some fabric and features from the medieval building remain. The church is entered through a squat W tower with thick walls, heavily buttressed and restored; the doorway with hollow chamfered pointed arch and jambs is possibly early 13th-century. The small Norman doorway to the nave, round-headed and with simple chamfered imposts, is the earliest remaining feature of the church. In the nave S wall is a two-light Decorated window of early 14th-century date; a single-light window from the same period has been restored and reset in the vestry. The timbered nave roof has crown-posts and tie-beams resting on old wall plates. The chancel, aisle and vestry date from the restoration. There are several 18th-century wall tablets; one commemorates a native of the Leeward Islands who, when fifteen years old, was brought to Madehurst by a Governor and remained as his servant until his death at the age of 67.

Vestry window

Maresfield *St Bartholomew* 42

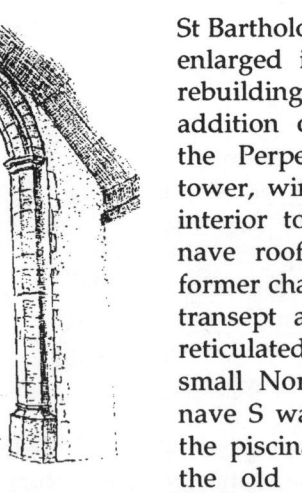
Tower arch

St Bartholomew's was greatly altered and enlarged in the 19th century with the rebuilding of the chancel and the addition of transepts. Remaining from the Perpendicular period are the W tower, window and doorway. The high interior tower arch rises almost to the nave roof. During the restoration the former chancel arch was re-sited in the N transept and the old E window, with reticulated tracery, in the S transept. A small Norman window remains in the nave S wall. Other medieval details are the piscina, two holy water stoups and the old font, a shallow bowl with fragments of its six supporting shafts.

The pulpit, which has a frieze of flat carving, and the balustered communion rail are Jacobean; even older woodwork is the N porch door frame which has carved spandrels and shafts. Over the N door are the carved and painted arms of George I. Interesting memorials include a cast iron slab (1667) and, outside, a number of 18th-century stone memorials in the style of wooden graveboards.

Mayfield *St Dunstan* 52

The Saxon Archbishop of Canterbury, St Dunstan, built a wooden church here in the 10th century. A later church was largely destroyed by fire in 1389; all that remains of it is the 13th-century tower (now with a shingled spire) and an Early English lancet at the W end of the N aisle. Rebuilding took place in the 15th and 16th centuries in the Perpendicular style. The nave has arcades of octagonal pillars with four-centred arches and a clerestory with Tudor arched windows. To the south is a chapel; the two-storeyed S porch has a vaulted roof. Between nave and chancel is a wooden arch with carved wooden infilling above. Among the furnishings are an octagonal font dated 1666, a carved Jacobean pulpit and, from the 18th century, the communion rail and two fine brass chandeliers. Memorials include cast iron tomb slabs, one of 1668 crudely lettered and another dated 1708 with a coat of arms. By the entrance is a carved and painted wall monument of 1602 with kneeling figures in Elizabethan costume. In the churchyard are several Harmer terracottas.

Brass chandelier

Merston *St Giles* 80W

The tiny village of Merston, three miles from Chichester, is quiet and remote; its 13th-century church stands among trees a short distance away. The roof on the N side covers nave and aisle and sweeps down almost to ground level; in the N wall is a door but no windows. Most

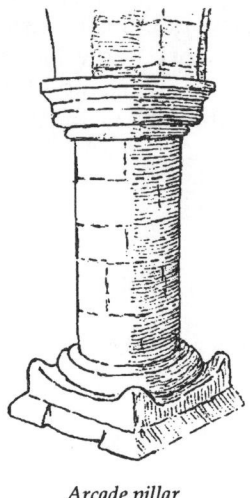

Arcade pillar

of the building is covered with modern roughcast. The 17th-century brick porch has a beam over the door with the inscription 'WI 1637 RI'. Undivided nave and chancel have lancet windows and are covered by a roof of tie-beams and crown-posts. The four-bay N arcade, probably early 14th-century, has round pillars with moulded bases and arches of two chamfered orders. In the W wall is a Perpendicular window of three trefoil-headed lights with tracery above; the aisle and chancel E windows are modern. In the chancel S wall is a shelved piscina; the communion rail with slender balusters is possibly 18th-century. The 12th-century square font stands on a central column surrounded by eight detached shafts; the top has been cut down leaving the sides with incomplete arcading.

Midhurst *St Mary Magdalene & St Denys* 82W

The church was once a chapel of the Priory of St Denys at Easebourne, nearby. Extensively restored in the 19th century, it is now a large town church. From the 16th century remain the upper part of the tower and the S aisle and chancel arcades. The oldest part of the church is the lower tower which is early 13th-century and has two Early English splayed lancets. Beneath the N arch is the octagonal font, probably Early English, on a pedestal of similar shape, both carved with uncusped arches. A rare feature of the tower clock is the two-second tick of its pendulum. There are 16th-century carved panels in the wooden pulpit and the church possesses a medieval chest with chip-carved roundels. In the chapel are the painted Royal Arms of Queen Anne.

Early English font

Mid Lavant *St Nicholas* 80W

The church, by the busy road north from Chichester, is a building much changed by the 19th and 20th centuries. The nave, with its tiny Norman window, dates from the 12th century, the chancel from the 13th. A N aisle and S porch were added in the 19th century, the N vestries in 1987. The interior was re-ordered in 1981 with the altar on the S side of the nave and seating around it. The Victorians built the chancel arches, sharply pointed on marble columns, to the north of which is a small 15th-century niche. The Early English chancel has old lancets in the N and S walls; the E window

Baroque monument

is modern. Below the string course the walls are unplastered and it can be seen that the SW lancet was once a low side window. There is foreign glass, possibly 17th-century, in some windows. Beneath the chancel is the vault of the May family, Lords of the Manor from the 16th to 18th centuries; engraved coffin plates from there are mounted on the W wall of the aisle. The notable monument to Dame Mary May (d.1681), sculpted by Bushnell, is in the Italian Baroque style. This was moved to the vault by 19th-century restorers but replaced in the church in 1987.

Milland *Old Church* 82W

Near the London-Portsmouth road is the Victorian church of St Luke with the old church behind it; an alternative approach is by footpath from the south up 75 stone steps. Built as a chapel of ease to Trotton, probably in the 16th century, the old church was originally a single room; a N transept, store and N porch were added in the 19th century. Outside steps by the S porch lead to the doorway, now blocked, of a former gallery. Exterior walls are stuccoed and the tiled roof has been

18th-century pulpit

renewed in recent times. Earlier this century the church functioned as a Sunday school but now is unused and dilapidated. Part of a three-decker 18th-century pulpit and a few box pews remain in the nave; on either side of the round-headed E window are wooden commandment, creed and prayer boards. In the S wall are two piscinae, one large and modern, the other small, square headed and possibly medieval. Large graveslabs of Sussex marble, their brasses removed, are set in the nave floor. The old font is now in the modern church.

Mountfield *All Saints* 72E

The small Norman church at Mountfield, in wooded countryside north of Battle, has a chancel and nave dating from the early 12th century.

Squint

The low W tower of two stages, built towards the end of that century, has a shingled broach spire. There is a 14th-century S porch with old timbers; the N vestry is modern. Original Norman features remain: two small round-headed windows and a blocked doorway in the nave N wall, the inner S doorway and the chancel arch, plain with cushion capitals. The large, circular font is also Norman with later decoration (fleurs-de-lis, foliage and shells) carved in the 16th century. Medieval wall painting around the chancel arch dates from more than one period, the most visible being the 13th-century masonry pattern with flowers, overpainted later with IHC monograms. The lancet windows and trefoil-headed piscina in the chancel are of the 13th century as are the squints on each side of the arch. The communion rail with moulded balusters dates from the 18th century. In the churchyard are two gravestones with Harmer terracotta plaques.

√ Newhaven *St Michael* 40

The name 'Newhaven' commemorates the making of the new harbour at the mouth of the Ouse after the river had been diverted from Seaford in the 16th century. To the west was the village of Meeching which, in time, was engulfed by its neighbour. Its Norman church (like many situated on hills, dedicated to St Michael) became the parish church of Newhaven. The 12th-century church had an uncommon design for this country: a central tower with nave to the west and apsidal chancel to the east. St Michael's now consists of the Norman apse and tower (with a later short spire) and a 19th-century nave. It is the old part that is special. From the east the church is seen almost as it was originally: the apse with narrow windows, the tower with twin arched belfry openings and corbel table. Within, the tiny apse is viewed through the dark tunnel of the tower arches, decorated with roll mouldings and supported on jambs with shafts and simple capitals.

Norman apse

Newick *St Mary the Virgin* ✓   42

The church is built of local stone, blocks of rust coloured sandstone for the tower and a sandstone rubble of lighter colours for the rest. The oldest part is the S wall of the nave which has one small round-headed Norman window. Most of the building however is of the 19th century when the nave was lengthened and a N aisle added. The 14th-century chancel was rebuilt at the end of the new nave; the porch of similar age was heightened but still retains some of its old timbers. The W tower dates from the 15th century, apart from the doorway, window and battlements that were added a century later. The 14th-century font, a square basin with ogee tracery, is mounted on a simple Norman base. In the tracery lights is old glass, contemporary with the chancel, depicting the Agnus Dei. The pulpit with sounding board is Jacobean.

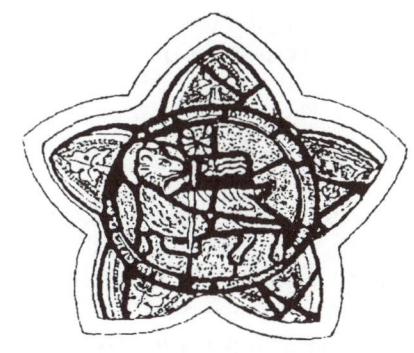

Agnus Dei

New Shoreham *St Mary de Haura* 20

St Mary's was built on a grand scale. In the 13th century it had a six-bay aisled nave, central tower with transepts and an aisled choir of five bays with triforium, clerestory and vaulted roof. At some time most of the Norman nave was demolished; one bay remains and now forms the entrance porch. This leads into the crossing beneath the tower and the lofty transepts with round-headed arches and some windows of c.1130. To the east is the choir, the lower levels of which are in the late 12th-century Transitional style. The aisle walls, decorated with blind arcades of round arches, have stone benches along their length. The choir arcades are the church's greatest distinction, the N arcade in particular. Alternate round and octagonal pillars have finely carved foliage capitals; the Transitional pointed arches are deeply moulded and also decorated with foliage. The S arcade, built slightly later, is quite different with compound pillars. The triforium openings have Transitional and Early English characteristics; the clerestory has Early English lancets.

Tower

Above the choir is quadripartite vaulting. The fine Norman font is of Sussex marble. A rare rood piscina remains high on the former nave wall. Outside are heavy flying buttresses, a large wheel window high in the E end above the vault level and, over all, the great tower spanning the styles of the 12th century.

Newtimber *St John the Baptist* 21

Newtimber is recorded in Domesday Book but there is no mention of a church. The present small church, set in fields with a few houses nearby, was built in the 13th century by the Lord of the Manor close to Newtimber Place. Most of the medieval parishioners would have come from the Saxon settlement at Saddlescombe. Heavily restored in the 19th century, it retains the basic structure of a simple, aisleless Early English church with mainly single lancet windows and a group of three in the E wall. A small N transept was once the manorial pew of Newtimber Place. The 19th-century tower replaces an earlier bell turret. The ten carved panels of the pulpit are Jacobean. Mounted on the wall near the modern font is a carved section of the medieval rood screen. In the tower are wooden commandment boards and an 18th-century cartouche commemorating members of the Osborne family. The 20th-century memorials tell a moving story of life and death, in peace and war, of a small community.

Cartouche

Ninfield *St Mary* 71E

The small church at Ninfield stands on high ground overlooking the Pevensey Levels and consists of a 13th-century nave, 17th-century chancel and, on the north, a modern aisle and vestry. A weatherboarded bell turret of c.1395 contains a bell of similar date. The brick S porch, added in 1735, has old wooden seats on stone corbels. Near the Perpendicular S doorway is the small square font with 17th-century carved oak cover. The ancient nave roof has moulded crown-posts and beams. At the W end is a 17th-century musicians' gallery, only accessible by ladder, with old banners hanging either side; the wavy balusters are 20th-century work. A small 17th-century brass (chancel S wall) commemorates infant daughters of John Bowyer, a former rector. The choir stalls are carved with fluted pilasters, flat arches and leaves and have interesting oak heads. Good examples of Jacobean work include a reader's desk, carved panelling (formerly the reredos and now placed in the N aisle) and the Royal Arms of James I. In the churchyard are early 18th-century gravestones.

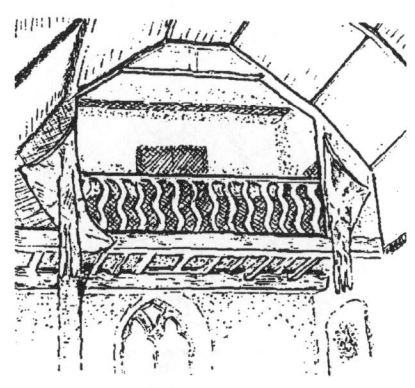

Musicians' gallery

Northiam *St Mary* 82E

Stone spire

Northiam is a Wealden village near the Kent border. St Mary's stands above the main street with its white weatherboarded houses. Remaining from the original 12th-century church is the lower part of the tower with thick walls of local ironstone. The tower is of four stages finished with a Perpendicular battlemented parapet and one of the three ancient stone spires in Sussex. Early in the 14th century aisles were added to the original nave and the S porch was built. The E end of the church is 19th-century as is the large mausoleum on the north. In the nave are three-bay N and S arcades; there is a clerestory with small windows. The tower has two small Norman windows, widely splayed. In each wall is a round arch; set into one is the pointed arch to the nave. The mausoleum contains memorials to the Frewen family, residents in Northiam since the 16th century. Reset in the chancel floor are several large graveslabs and two early 16th-century brasses to a priest and a civilian. Above the W door are the Royal Arms of Queen Anne dated 1713. Furnishings include an 18th-century pulpit and a brass chandelier dated 1727. Preserved from the former chancel are the communion rail, the altar table and oak panelling round it, all given by Thankful Frewen in 1638.

North Marden *St Mary* 81W

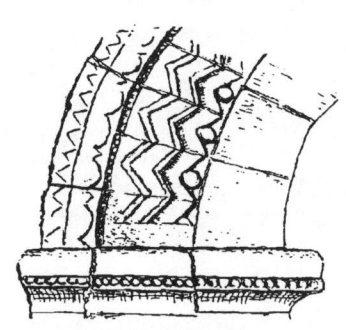

South doorway (detail)

The Mardens were, until this century, small parishes in the rolling, wooded Downland at the western end of Sussex; now they have been combined into larger units. North Marden was a very small community of farms, a manor and a church; it remains the same today. The small 12th-century church is set in fields beside a farmyard and consists of a single chamber with apsidal east end to which a modern S porch and N vestry have been added. In the 19th century it was restored and a bell turret built with a tiled pyramidal roof. High up in the W gable is an original round-headed Norman window; other windows are modern though in ancient style. The S doorway within the porch is of the 12th century with chevron and pellet ornament. St Mary's has one of the five medieval apses in Sussex and is one of the few churches remaining in the country with this apsidal single chamber plan.

North Mundham *St Stephen* 80W

The village lies on the coastal plain east of Chichester. St Stephen's dates from the 13th century, to which period belong the aisled nave and some details in the W tower (the reset W door with nook shafts and the belfry windows). There is evidence from local wills that the tower was built (or rebuilt) in the 16th century. The top stage is finished with a projecting cornice and battlements, similar to the 16th-century tower at nearby Donnington. The rest of the church dates from the 19th century. Incorporated in the modern S porch is a worn carving, part of a 16th-century memorial. The nave arcades of Caen stone are in typical Early English style: circular pillars, moulded capitals, bases with spurs and double-chamfered pointed arches. In the central aisle are ledger slabs of the 18th century, some with small inscribed brasses. By the blocked N doorway is the imposing font, a massive circular bowl (possibly 12th-century) with straight sides and moulding beneath, standing on a modern fluted base.

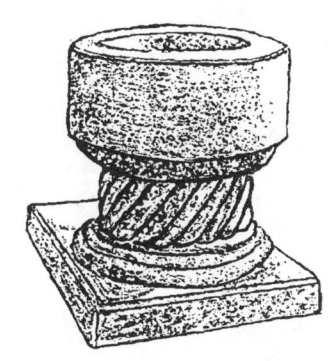

Font

North Stoke  01

The tiny hamlet of North Stoke can be approached along a dead-end road from Houghton, by footpath across the river Arun from South Stoke or over the Downs from Burpham. Its spacious, cruciform

Stained glass

church has a timeless atmosphere scarcely disturbed by restoration. Windows in the nave reveal its Norman origins, while others throughout the church show the development of medieval window design. There are Early English lancets in the chancel and windows with a variety of Decorated tracery in the transepts. The elaborately moulded chancel arch (of clunch) has flanking niches, one (N) with a hand carved on a corbel. Above the arch are remains of 14th-century wall paintings. Image brackets either side of the chancel E window are carved with foliage and tiny faces. A small, exquisite, stained glass panel (c. 1300) depicts the Coronation of the Virgin. The piscina and triple sedilia are connected by continuous roll moulding. An unusual feature in the W wall of the S transept is a recess surmounted by two tall arches joining in a grotesque corbel. The bowl-shaped font of Pulborough stone dates from the 13th century. In the churchyard (SE), three tapering graveslabs carved with crosses are probably late 13th-century.

Nuthurst *St Andrew* 12

Nuthurst lies in a secluded Wealden valley four miles from Horsham. The sandstone church, roofed with Horsham slabs, has undergone several restorations and from the south appears almost entirely Victorian. However, on the N side is the original 12th-century chancel wall which has a small Norman window with incised zig-zag decoration. The nave, built in the early 14th century, has pairs of cusped lancets; from the internal buttresses westwards is the Victorian extension which, with the shingled bell turret, replaced a former W tower. Many fittings were renewed and the N vestry was built during this major restoration completed

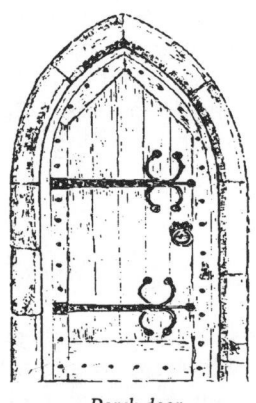
Porch door

in 1907. The oldest part of the church is the chancel, enlarged in the 13th or 14th century; in the E window tracery is old glass showing Christ in Majesty and angels with censers. On a window sill is a brass dated 1486 to Thomas Ffenshe, a former rector. The church has a dugout chest and a 15th-century dole cupboard which stand in the nave; also of interest are the old hinges on the porch and vestry doors.

Old Shoreham *St Nicolas*  20

Before the Adur valley silted up, the harbour and centre of population were at Old Shoreham. Its sturdy, cruciform church is recorded in Domesday Book and, although the main features are Norman, its origins are pre-Conquest. Part of the nave N wall is of that period; a blocked arch near the NW corner once led into a Saxon tower which can be traced in the present building. The central Norman tower is c.1140; at the belfry stage it has three arches and two circular openings on each side, unusual in this country. Original Norman work includes the shallow buttresses on the N and S walls of the transepts and the S transept doorway. Inside, the four Norman arches beneath the tower are carved with a remarkable variety of ornament including chevron with pellets, cable with beads, stud, lozenge and rose, billet and limpet. On the N arch are faces of a king and queen, possibly Stephen and his consort; there is a cat face on the nave arch. The Early English chan-

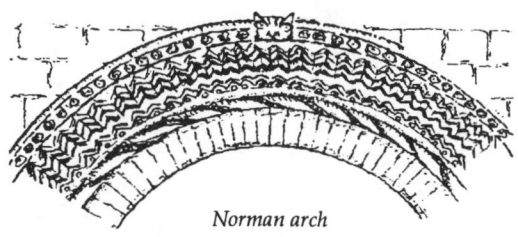
Norman arch

cel is entered through an oak screen of c.1300 (much restored) and contemporary with it is the moulded and carved tie-beam which has original colouring. Even older is the rare Norman tie-beam in the nave. For many years the church was in ruins; there is a detailed account of its condition and restoration in 1839-40.

Oving *St Andrew* 90W

Oving is on the fertile coastal plain east of Chichester. Its large church of chancel, nave, transepts and W tower with broach spire dates almost entirely from the 13th century. The roofs, N porch and S vestry are the

Chancel arch corbel

result of 19th-century restoration. Most windows in the flint walls are Early English lancets; two three-light windows in the nave are 14th-century and the E window is modern. A feature of distinction is the 14th-century N doorway carved from clunch. This has a moulded arch with foliage label stops and on either side are nook shafts with nailhead decoration around the capitals. The interior is spacious due to the wide aisleless nave and high chancel arch. Decorated corbels, scalloped and moulded, supporting the inner order of the arch are similar to those in other 13th-century churches of the area. The N transept, now a chapel, has an ancient altar stone with consecration crosses, found during the Victorian restoration. Above the S door are the carved Royal Arms of Queen Victoria.

Ovingdean St Wulfran 30

The Domesday Book records a church at Ovingdean described as an 'ecclesiola' but authorities disagree as to whether this is part of the present church or not. There are no obvious Saxon features. The nave and chancel are Norman and the W tower, with lancet windows and Sussex cap, of the late 12th century. A former S aisle may have been destroyed by fire; the arches and discoloured stones can be seen in the exterior S wall. In the nave N wall is the original Norman doorway (blocked) with a stoup beside it. Also of this period is the plain chancel arch and a small round window above (the flanking arches are modern). An opening in the chancel S wall leads to a modern chapel. There is a 14th-century rood screen, now positioned behind the altar. The chancel ceiling, the rood and most of the stained glass are by Charles Kempe; a large tomb in the churchyard, a memorial to members of his family, was designed by him. The dedication to St Wulfran is rare in England; there is one other at Grantham in Lincolnshire.

Blocked doorway

Pagham *St Thomas à Becket* 89W

Excavations in 1976 uncovered remains of a small Saxon church. From an 11th-century Norman church are the nave foundations, the NW tower and parts of the chancel (see the herringbone masonry in the S wall) but the present building, of flint with stone dressings is mainly 13th-century. There was substantial 19th-century rebuilding; the Norman style W wall is all Victorian and the aisles and transepts were largely rebuilt in the Early English style, as was the chancel arch. The oldest visible parts inside are the Transitional nave arcades of c.1200 with round pillars, stiff-leaf carving and pointed arches. The 13th-century chancel has single lancets in the N and S walls; a string course below forms the lintel of

Stained glass

a flat-topped piscina. The E wall has triple lancets with dogtooth ornament and nook-shafts; there is 16th-century Flemish stained glass in the lower panels. A stained glass shield in the N aisle depicts the instruments of the Passion. The 12th-century square font has shallow arcading and a four-lobed foliage design. In the mortar of the exterior walls are insertions of flint chips, a practice known as galleting. The churchyard has fine 18th-century carved gravestones.

Parham *St Peter* 01

St Peter's stands near the Elizabethan house in Parham Park; it was once surrounded by village houses but these were demolished in the late 18th century. The church is built of local stone and is largely a rebuilding of 1800-1820 when the tower was added. Unaltered by the restoration is the S chancel chapel (now the vestry) which was remodelled in 1545 as directed under the will of Robert Palmer, to whom Henry VIII granted Parham manor. Medieval walls of an earlier church are evident in the SE corner of the chapel.

Squire's pew

A blocked two-bay arcade in the nave N wall is probably medieval also. The high box pews and barrel ceiling were installed about 1800; the oak communion rail and part of the chancel screen date from the 18th century. North of the chancel is the squire's pew with a separate entrance porch, panelled plaster ceiling and a fireplace. The rare lead font, one of three in Sussex, dates from the mid 14th century. The small circular bowl has the inscription 'IHC Nazar' repeated horizontally and vertically in Lombardic lettering, a unique decoration. Also on the bowl are the arms of Andrew Peverell, Knight, 1351.

Patcham All Saints

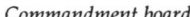

Commandment board

Patcham, on the northern outskirts of Brighton, retains some of its village identity, especially near the church. All Saints' consists of a W tower, nave, chancel, and S porch; a N aisle, vestry and short spire were added in the 19th century. There are massive buttresses to tower and nave. The walls are covered with cement and only the windows give an indication of age: 13th-century lancets in the tower and 14th-century Decorated windows in nave and chancel. From the inside its even greater age is apparent; the 12th-century chancel arch is flanked by round-headed recesses and in the N aisle is a reset doorway, Norman or possibly earlier. Above the chancel arch is a Doom painting of c.1230, uncovered in the 19th century. The roof has old tie-beams, queen-posts and boarded rafters. Engraved commandment, creed and prayer tablets are mounted on the W wall. Recently the church was re-ordered with the altar in front of the chancel arch. In the chancel are N and S low side windows and an E window of intersecting tracery with foliated lights. A memorial of 1594 to Richard Shelley has carvings of gravediggers. The piscina is 14th-century. In the churchyard are 18th-century chest tombs carved with angels and skulls and, on the N side, a memorial to a smuggler 'unfortunately shot'.

Patching *St John the Divine*

St John's is mainly a simple Early English church of nave, chancel, S porch and N tower. The 13th-century tower has arches opening to the east into a chapel/vestry, to the west into a small porch and to the south into the nave. Throughout the church the windows are single lancets; the E wall has two lancets with a small circular light above. The fine 15th-century font is octagonal with quatrefoil decoration; the pulpit has some Renaissance carved panels. The trefoil piscina and double sedilia in the chancel are restored but contain early work. In the 17th century when the structure was in a state of disrepair the nave was largely rebuilt. During the 19th century the walls were re-faced, the shingled broach spire constructed and previously inserted Perpendicular windows replaced by Early English style lancets. The simple 13th-century appearance is therefore to some extent the result of Victorian restoration.

Pulpit

Peasmarsh *St Peter & St Paul*

The church stands in parkland near Peasmarsh Place, away from the village. It consists of a chancel, nave with aisles, W tower with shingled spire and modern N vestry. The tower, supported by short clasping buttresses, is late 12th-century; also from this period is the lancet at the W end of the N aisle. Transitional arcades in the nave have square pillars, chamfered abaci and pointed arches. Features remaining from an earlier Norman church are the blocked window high in the W wall and the round-headed chancel arch. The arch is constructed of ironstone blocks and has, below the imposts, carvings of animals biting their tails. Other carvings of similar age are reset in the exterior walls. The chancel, rebuilt in the 13th century, has narrow lancets, piscina and

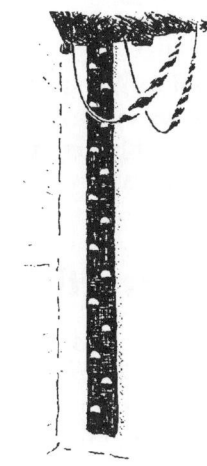
Belfry ladder

sedilia and a 14th-century low side window. Above the chancel arch are commandment tables painted on plaster. There is a charity board in the tower; a vertical plank with semicircular footholds gives access to the belfry.

Penhurst *St Michael*   61

Church, manor house and farm buildings form a picturesque hilltop group in thinly populated countryside near Battle. In the 19th century the church, then dilapidated, was restored but little altered. Built of Wealden sandstone, it dates from the 14th century as do the nave windows, all of two lights with trefoil heads under square labels. The W tower is 15th-century and the N chapel, originally built as a private pew, is 17th-century. There are two entrances, one by a S porch with medieval woodwork. The other is through the buttressed tower which has a large three-light Perpendicular window and is tile hung below its pyramidal roof. On the N wall inside are prayer, creed, commandment and text boards. A high arch opens to the nave which has a crown-post roof, panelled walls and box pews; there is a squint north of the chancel arch. The chancel has a wagon roof and, in the S wall, a priest's doorway and a piscina. Fragments of medieval glass in the E window show canopies, angels and shields. Old furnishings are retained in the church: the 15th-century oak screen between nave and chancel, the 17th-century communion rail with turned balusters and the Jacobean pulpit and reader's desk. The font, octagonal in bowl and stem, is 15th-century.

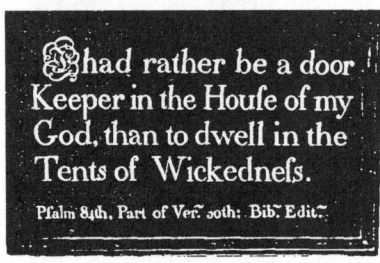

Text board

Petworth *St Mary*   92W

Petworth is an attractive town of winding streets and old houses adjacent to the famous Petworth estate. The church dates from the 13th century but is so altered and restored that little ancient work is visible. Dominating the exterior is the fine, large tower, the result of three construction periods. The stone base is 14th-century, the upper part of brick was built by Sir Charles Barry in the 19th century and the parapet and pyramidal cap date from 1953. Inside, the nave N arcade has 14th-century arches; the chancel is 13th-century with windows of two lights beneath a roundel (S wall). All woodwork is modern. Under the tower is the 14th-century font, octagonal and carved with quatrefoils. On the walls are prayer, creed and commandment boards and an oval relief of the Virgin and Child by Flaxman. At the W end of the church are the Royal Arms of George III, moulded in Coade stone. Among the many memorials is an altar tomb to Sir John Dawtry (d.1542) and

Virgin and Child

his wife with their kneeling figures and coats of arms. A monument to John Wickens (d.1783), a former rector, has an early carving by Flaxman of a cherub floating on clouds.

Pevensey St Nicholas 60

The church lies east of the Roman fort and later Norman castle. It is basically a 13th-century church with aisled nave, chancel and N tower. Considerable restoration in the 19th century provided the upper stage of the tower, the N chapel and porch. The interior is uniformly Early English in style. The S arcade of five bays has steeply pointed arches supported by pillars alternately quatrefoil and octagonal. The N arcade has three similar bays and an opening into the tower. The tower arch corbels are carved, one with a coiled tress of hair, several with heads. The chancel arch,

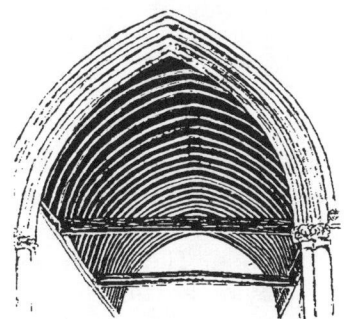

Chancel roof

again steeply pointed, has stiff-leaf capitals and opens into a long chancel which has two arched openings at the W end, probably late 12th-century and part of an earlier church. At the E end are triple lancets, in the S wall a fine pair of lancets with hoodmoulds, carved heads and decorative shafts. In the S aisle are two medieval graveslabs with crosses. Of the two fonts, one is modern, the other medieval, a square block of stone. In the N aisle is an alabaster monument to John Wheatley (d.1616) in the classical style with the effigy reclining between Corinthian columns and allegorical female figures.

Piddinghoe 40

The 12th-century flint church at Piddinghoe near Newhaven is on a mound beside the river Ouse. Its round tower, one of three in Sussex, is Norman and has six round-headed belfry openings; the low shingled spire has a large weathervane in the shape of a salmon trout. Originally the church consisted of nave and tower only; by the mid 12th century the N aisle was added followed shortly by a S aisle. The chancel is early 13th-century. Chancel aisles were built but later demolished as was the nave S aisle. All were rebuilt in a restoration of 1882; the clerestory and porch date from this time. Inside are interesting architectural features. The N arcade with unmoulded round arches is Norman; the aisle wall is original though with 14th-century windows. Built c.1200, the S arcade has pointed arches, slightly chamfered; the simple tower arch is round without imposts. From the Early English period is the fine chancel arch on triple shafts with stiff-leaf carving on the capitals. The E wall has three stepped lancets, deeply recessed with inner roll mouldings, and an oculus in the gable. Most of the stained glass and furnishings were installed during the restoration. The square green sandstone font is 13th-century. In the churchyard are the village stocks with the original stone supports.

Tower

Playden St Michael 92E

Playden is a mile north of Rye on a wooded ridge overlooking Romney Marsh. St Michael's is an almost complete church of the late 12th century with chancel, central tower, nave and two aisles extending to enclose the tower. The nave arcades, of four bays, have Transitional pillars, alternately round and octagonal; three arches are round, the westernmost pointed. Round windows from a former clerestory can be seen, one each side above the arches, but they are now covered by a steep roof over both nave and aisles. In the N aisle is a single original window, narrow and round-headed in a deep splay. The chancel was partly rebuilt in the 16th century and the E window, under a four-centred arch, is of this period. There is woodwork of great interest: a massive wooden ladder of uncertain age giving access to the belfry, a Perpendicular screen of the 15th century under the E arch of the tower and, finest of all, a screen of c.1310 under the N tower arch, carved with flamboyant tracery in the continental style. In the N aisle is a rare tomb slab of a brewer with a Flemish inscription and carvings showing the implements of his trade. Rising above the tower is a slender broach spire, tall enough to be seen over the trees.

Parclose screen, c.1310

Plumpton St Michael

An earlier church at Plumpton was recorded in the Domesday Book; the present building of flint with Sussex marble and sandstone dressings, dates from 1100. The nave and S doorway are Norman, the chancel and W tower are 13th-century and there is a 16th-century brick porch. A shingled broach spire rises above the squat tower which has just one belfry window (N); the buttresses and W doorway are of the 14th century. In the 19th century the chancel E wall was rebuilt and a N vestry added. Of particular interest are the medieval wall paintings discovered in 1955. These belong to the Clayton, Coombes and Hardham group and are high on the nave N wall; others above the chancel arch were destroyed during the Victorian restoration. Binoculars are useful when viewing the paintings which show (from E to W) Christ seated in the New Jerusalem, scroll decoration in the splay of a Norman

Norman window

window and St Peter carrying a key. On the W wall are 18th-century commandment, creed and prayer boards. There are Jacobean choir stalls in the chancel; old box pews have been used to line the nave roof.

Poling St Nicholas   00

The ancient village of Poling lies on the coastal plain near Arundel. Its church has Saxon origins and the nave walls remain from this period.

15th-century brass

The chancel was completely rebuilt c.1380; there are re-used Saxon stones at the E end. The 15th-century tower has angle buttresses and square-headed bell-openings. Inside, a two-bay nave arcade gives onto a 13th-century aisle built by the Knights Hospitallers, then established here. The Saxon double-splayed window in the nave N wall was uncovered earlier this century; part of its oak shutter was still in place and is displayed below. The tub-shaped font may be Saxon though the pedestal is later. On the roof tie-beams are elaborately carved wooden bosses from the Fitzalan chapel, Arundel. Above the tower arch are the painted Royal Arms of George I, dated 1714. Between nave and chancel is a 14th-century screen, (restored) with a battlemented rood beam above. On the chancel floor is a 15th-century brass to Walter Davy, a former vicar, a tonsured demi-figure wearing a chasuble. Near the S door is an unusual iron poor box of uncertain date. A gravestone in the porch dated 1740 has an inscription which ends: 'If Life was a thing/ That money could buy/ The Rich would live/ And the Poor would dye'.

Portslade St Nicholas   20

After centuries as a Downland village overlooking the sea, Portslade is now part of the Brighton conurbation surrounded by industry and housing. St Nicholas' however, with the manor and old flint walls nearby, retains the character of a country church. It has a 13th-century W tower of rubble with stone quoins and a later battlemented top, a nave and chancel with Horsham slab roofs and lancet windows. Inside, the church's earlier history is apparent. The Transitional S arcade has round pillars, scalloped capitals and high bases with corner spurs. This opens onto a typically narrow 12th-century aisle in which the windows are 13th and 14th-century replacements. The 16th-century memorial brass was found in the ruins of West Blatchington church.

Piscina and sedilia

In the chancel E wall are two lancets with a sex-foil window above. There are triple sedilia and a piscina under moulded arches; in the floor are 18th-century ledger slabs. Commandment tablets in the tower date from the 18th century. The N aisle and NW chapel are 19th-century additions, the arcade being a Victorian copy of the one to the south.

Poynings *Holy Trinity*

The top of Newtimber hill gives a fine view of Poynings under the scarp slope of the South Downs; prominent is the large church with its massive central tower. Rebuilt completely in the 14th century under the will of Michael de Poynings, it is an early Perpendicular structure faced with knapped flint under a Horsham slab roof. The N porch of squared flints was built slightly later. The spacious nave, large chancel and transepts radiate from the crux of the building, the strong crossing arches beneath the tower. Although rescued from a dilapidated state in the 19th century, the church is not obviously restored and has an imposing simplicity. Among original fittings are the triple sedilia and piscina (ogee arched under a flat head) and probably the octagonal font (bowl and stem of the same width with trefoil arches on the sides). There are fragments of 15th-century stained glass with two figures high in the tracery lights of the

Font

N transept. The S transept is entered through a medieval screen. Other woodwork of note includes a Jacobean carved pulpit, box pews and a three-sided communion rail of the 17th century.

Preston *St Peter* 30

Preston village is now part of Brighton; the church stands on rising ground by the manor near the main London Road. Apart from a modern porch and vestry, St Peter's is entirely 13th-century. The chancel, long nave and thin tower are of flint with stone dressings. High in the tower are small lancets below a corbel table carved with masks which supports a pyramidal cap. The aisleless nave has three windows in each side as does the chancel, broad lancets deeply splayed. The chancel, entered through a pointed arch of Caen stone, has triple sedilia with trefoil arches and jamb shafts; the adjacent piscina has two bowls and a shelf. The altar is, unusually, a tomb chest, that of Edward Eldrington who held the nearby manor and died in 1515. It is finely carved with shields in cusped quatrefoils. A fire in 1906 caused serious damage to the once extensive medieval wall paintings in the nave; three remaining fragments depict the Nativity, the Martyrdom of St Thomas Becket and St Michael weighing souls. The church is now cared for by the Redundant Churches Fund.

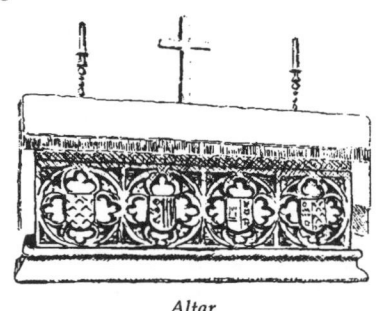

Altar

Pulborough *St Mary* 01

Entrance to the churchyard is through an ancient lychgate roofed with Horsham slabs. Two main building styles are represented in the church; the chancel, built c.1220, is Early English while the nave, aisles, tower and N porch date from the 15th-century Perpendicular period. Windows are tall lancets in the chancel and of two lights with cinquefoil heads and vertical tracery in the aisles; the clerestory windows match the tower bell-openings. Inside, the fine four-bay arcades have pillars with attached shafts and moulded capitals and bases. In the chancel, which has a pronounced inclination to the north, are 14th-century piscina and triple sedilia. The E window is of three lancets under an arch with roll moulding and nook-shafts. A two-bay arcade gives onto a N chapel with a Perpendicular canopied tomb chest. A brass in the N aisle commemorates Thomas Harlyng (d.1423), a former rector. Two other 15th-century brasses are in the S aisle where the E window, two trefoil lights and a quatrefoil, survives from the mid 14th century. The 12th-century font is of Purbeck marble, a square bowl with carved arcading. In the tower are the painted Royal Arms of George III.

Aisle window

Pyecombe *The Transfiguration of our Lord* 21

The flint church at Pyecombe stands on the southern slope of Wolstonbury hill, six miles north of Brighton. It dates from the 12th century; the low tower was added in the early 13th century. Entrance to the churchyard is through a tapsell gate fitted with a Pyecombe crook, familiar to many Downland shepherds. A N porch roofed with Horsham slabs leads to an aisleless nave and chancel separated by triple arches; the outer openings are modern, the central arch, unmoulded and on plain imposts, is Norman. Above are the Royal Arms of George III together with commandment, creed and prayer boards. The pulpit carries its date (1636) and has ornamental flat carving of the period similar to that on the Rector's stall opposite. In the chancel is a double piscina (c.1300) under an ogee arch. The Early English lancets were renewed during a 19th-century restoration; the nave windows date from c.1500. A notable possession of the church is its lead font, one of only three in Sussex. It is of the 12th century, large and drum-shaped with ornament that includes fluting, trefoil arcading and a wide main band of double scrolls under arches.

Lead font

Racton

70W

Racton church is west of Funtington, close to the road with a few houses but no village. Small and simple, it has chancel and nave with a W bell turret and modern porch. The nave is 12th-century but its W wall was rebuilt in the 14th century in chequered flint and ashlar. The 13th-century chancel retains one original lancet window (S); the windows in the E and W walls are Perpendicular. Still with its original hinges, an old entrance door opens to the attractive interior. Marking the division between nave and chancel is a massive tie-beam with the Royal Arms of George II and wooden tracery above. The trussed rafter nave roof is ancient and the font probably 12th-century. In the chancel are commandment boards, a medieval aumbry and three monuments, diverse in date and style. The earliest, a 16th-century canopied table tomb, has panels carved with swans and putti and a bas-relief of the kneeling family facing a central figure of Christ. Recently repainted is the memorial to Sir George Gunter (d.1624) and his wife with standing figures of Justice and Charity. The bust of Sir Charles Nicholl (d.1733) is set in an architectural frame of black and white marble. Displayed above is armour which, following the custom of the time, was carried in the funeral procession.

Funeral armour

Ringmer St Mary

40

Of the original Norman church at Ringmer little remains apart from architectural fragments built into the SW buttress and, inside, the massive bases of the nave pillars. The present church is an interesting mixture of building styles, having a Decorated nave, a Perpendicular chancel, early Tudor chapels and a Victorian W tower. The exterior exhibits a variety of materials including flint, sandstone, bricks and Isle of White greenstone in the walls under roofs of Horsham slabs and tiles. A restored S porch contains original timbers and leads to an aisled nave with 14th-century arcades. Separating the chancel from the chapels are Perpendicular arcades with four-centred arches; the chancel E window is a 19th-century replacement. The S chapel was built c.1500, though its S window and doorway date from the 14th century. Several memorials here are to the Springett family; an alabaster tablet with a kneeling figure between obelisks is dated 1620. The N chapel with its fine E window was built about 35 years later than the S chapel. It has a Jacobean ceiling with painted beams. Memorials include brasses and an undated alabaster tablet with kneeling figures.

Chapel window, c.1500

Ripe *St John the Baptist*    51

This is an imposing church for a small village. Built of flint and sandstone, it has a late 13th-century nave and S porch, a 14th-century chancel and 15th-century W tower. The large nave is lit by four later windows of the Perpendicular period. At the E end are the remains of staircase and doorway to a former rood loft. The chancel arch frames the the late Decorated E window which has five lights with elaborate curvilinear tracery and contains pieces of 14th and 15th-century stained glass. In the chancel are sedile and piscina with moulded pointed arches. The tower is a massive structure of sandstone blocks with diagonal buttresses, battlements and a tiled pyramidal cap. The W doorway has label stops carved with the Pelham buckle. There are several of these 'Pelham towers' in villages neighbouring the family seat at Laughton.

Rood loft stairway

Rodmell *St Peter*    40

There was a Domesday church at Rodmell but the present building dates from the 12th century when it belonged to Lewes Priory. The nave, chancel and S chapel are from the mid-century, the S aisle, W tower and attached baptistery from about fifty years later. The N vestry and S porch were added in the 19th century. An impressive interior feature is the two-bay nave arcade; this has simple round arches supported by a massive cylindrical pillar with a square abacus, stiff-leaf carving and corner corbels (similar to those at Beddingham and St Anne's, Lewes). The 19th-century chancel arch has Norman chevron ornament copied from an earlier arch, thought to have been constructed in the 16th century of stones from the ruins of Lewes Priory. Windows vary in age and style: Norman, Decorated and Perpendicular. Several, like those in the nave N wall, are Victorian; one of these, a small quatrefoil above the pulpit, contains rare 15th-century stained glass of the Trinity. The square Norman font is carved with shallow arcading. Also of interest are the painted Royal Arms of George III, a 14th-century parclose screen and a small brass. The latter, originally from a 15th-century memorial, has been used on the reverse side for a 17th-century inscription.

Arcade pillar

Rogate *St Bartholomew* 82W

Rogate is near the Hampshire border and its church, built of local sandstone, stands in the centre of the village. In the 19th century the nave was extended, tower and vestry added and the exterior walls of aisles and chapels were rebuilt. Despite this extensive restoration, interior medieval features remain. The nave arcades have circular pillars and square abaci. One arch (N) is round and is the oldest surviving part of the building (c.1150). Except for the westernmost arches, the others are 13th-century, slightly pointed and double-chamfered. Also from this period are the chancel arch, piscina and triple sedilia in the S wall. The cinquefoil-headed window above and the arch to the N chapel date from the 14th century. In the N wall is an aumbry and a 15th-century square-headed two-light window. An impressive feature is

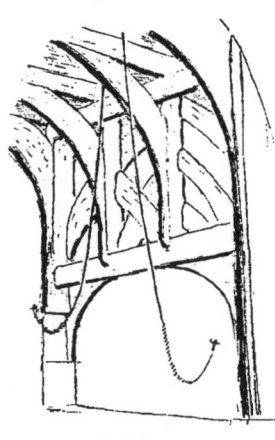
Bell frame

the medieval bell-frame which originally stood between the present central arches of the nave arcades. This massive structure of huge Wealden oak beams was dismantled in 1874 and rebuilt on a new stone base in the tower.

Rotherfield *St Denys* 52

Rotherfield church in the High Weald is a sandstone building dating mainly from the 13th century. Perpendicular additions include the battlemented tower with stair turret; its timber-framed spire, blown down in the 1987 hurricane, has since been rebuilt. The 15th-century N entrance porch has rib vaulting and a room above. Immediately inside the church is an iron graveslab with raised cross but no inscription, probably pre-Reformation. A wagon roof covers the nave which has three-bay arcades; the earlier N arcade has round pillars while on the south the pillars are octagonal. Substantial areas of medieval wall painting were uncovered in the 19th century; a Doom above the chancel arch depicts Christ seated on a rainbow surrounded by angels and monks. St Michael, one wing uplifted, is weighing souls. The fine 17th-century canopied pulpit is elaborately carved with geometrical patterns and eagles in profile. An octagonal font cover, dated 1533, has the carved coat of arms of George Nevill, then Lord of the Manor. Box pews, tiered at the W end, are 19th-century. The chancel has tall lancet windows; the Perpendicular E window contains glass made by William Morris from a design by Edward Burne-Jones. The sedilia and piscina (S wall) date from the 13th century. In the Nevill chapel are fragments of 14th-century stained glass.

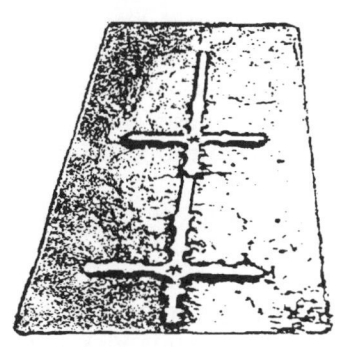

Iron graveslab

Rottingdean *St Margaret*  30

Rottingdean was a Saxon settlement recorded in the Domesday Book. The church is built on rising ground in the centre of the coastal village near Brighton. It is believed that a pre-Conquest church stood on the

13th-century tower

site of the present one, though there are no obviously Saxon features. The subsequent 12th-century Norman church was built by William de Warenne and from this remains the nave N wall. Its central tower collapsed within about a century and the present 13th-century tower was built; this has three levels of tall Early English lancets and is heavily buttressed. The chancel dates from the same period and retains the original priest's doorway in the S wall. A second catastrophe occurred in the 14th century when French raiders set fire to the church causing great destruction. An extensive restoration took place in the 19th century. There are seven stained glass windows set in the chancel and tower lancets. These were designed by former Rottingdean resident, Sir Edward Burne-Jones, and made by the William Morris workshop.

Rudgwick Holy Trinity 03

Situated on a Wealden ridge at the northern edge of the county, the church at Rudgwick is only a few metres from Surrey; the Sussex Border Path crosses the churchyard. The oldest part is the early 13th-century tower, built of roughly coursed sandstone and finished with a corbel table beneath a shingled pyramidal cap. Massive clasping buttresses dominate the W side; between them is the W doorway beneath a later 14th-century three-light window. Apart from the modern vestry and S porch the rest of the church, roofed with Horsham slabs, is early 14th-century. The spacious interior has high tower and chancel arches and a three-bay arcade giving onto a wide N aisle. The building has refined architectural detail; octagonal pillars and abaci support arcade arches of two moulded orders, tall two-light windows have Geometrical tracery of various designs and, in the aisle, small carved heads as label

Clasping buttresses

stops. A low priest's doorway in the chancel has a high inner arch with a hoodmould; a piscina to the east and an aumbry in the N wall are beneath crocketed gables. The 17th-century wooden altar table came from a church in Belgium. The late 12th-century font (restored), a square bowl of Sussex marble, has round-headed arcading.

Rusper *St Mary Magdalene* 23

In the 13th century a small settlement of nuns was established at Rusper (see the plaque on the exterior S wall). The medieval church was probably founded about this time but was rebuilt in the 19th century except for the tower. This substantial Perpendicular structure of local Wealden stone has heavy buttresses and a square stair turret on the SE corner. During the rebuilding its height was increased by about 3m, old stones being re-used for the alteration. The timber-framed porch is 16th-century. By the entrance is an ancient iron-bound chest with three locks and an old font not now in use. Above the tower arch to the nave are the carved and painted Royal Arms of George I. The brass chandelier hanging in the central aisle is a fine example of 18th-century craftsmanship. Reset in the chancel (N wall) are interesting brasses; one dated 1532 is to Thomas Challoner and his wife and an earlier one, c.1370, to John de Kingsfold, has demi-figures and an inscription in Norman French.

Perpendicular tower

Rustington *St Peter & St Paul* 00

Rustington church is notable for its architectural detail of the late 12th and early 13th centuries. The Transitional tower has lancets in the lower stage and bell-openings of two round-headed lights under a pointed arch. Seen on entering through the N door is the fine Transitional S arcade. The pillars are alternately round and octagonal, the capitals have both scalloped and waterleaf decoration and the arches, just pointed, rest on square abaci. Arches to the N transeptal chapel and chancel are of slightly later date with more pointed arches

Transitional arcade

but with simple square imposts. A feature of the chancel is the S priest's doorway with a small recess to the west, possibly a low side window or an opening to an anchorite's cell. From the 14th century are the clerestory quatrefoils and the two arches of the N arcade. In the chapel is a long squint to the chancel and there are stairs to a former rood loft. On view in the tower is the working mechanism of the 18th-century one-handed tower clock.

Rye St Mary   92E

One of the largest churches in Sussex, St Mary's consists of a nave with aisles, central tower with transepts and a chancel with N and S chapels. There are remains of a mid 12th-century Norman church: wall arcading in the transepts and reliquary recesses in the chancel E wall. The five-bay Transitional nave arcades have massive pillars with moulded capitals and bases; the arches, more pointed toward the W end, have hoodmoulds with dogtooth decoration. The chapels are 13th-century with lancet windows; the thick walls contain passages at the sill level. Town and church were set on fire in the French raid of 1377; the tower and part of the chancel collapsed. The chancel arcades retain two of the original 13th-century pillars and arches, the rest being replacements; flying buttresses support the E end. Above the chancel arch are the Royal Arms of Queen Anne dated 1704. The low tower has battlements and a short spire carrying a golden weathervane, visible for miles from the sea and the flat marshland. Mounted outside on the N transeptal entrance is the 18th-century church clock, its painted and gilded frame incorporating two figures (quarter boys) which strike bells at the quarter hours. The clock is driven by a 16th-century mechanism and has an 18 ft pendulum visible inside the church.

Flying buttress

Salehurst *St Mary*

Salehurst, six miles north of Battle, has a large church for so small a village but originally it served a more extensive parish including, probably, Etchingham and Bodiam. The chancel, nave and lower tower date from c.1250 and the aisle walls, N chapel and upper tower from about a century later. All are in Hastings sandstone. Windows range from Early English lancets to a variety of Decorated styles. There is a fine timber S porch c.1350 and an imposing W porch of stone with vaulted roof. The tower is notable for its great height and its top with chamfered corners. The need for the W buttresses is apparent on entering the church; the tower has no solid walls at ground level and is supported by four massive piers. East of the tower is the long nave with six-bay arcades of octagonal pillars. Both clerestory and roof were rebuilt in the 19th century. The font, beneath the tower, has a base encircled by carved salamanders; tradition maintains that it was presented by Richard I, which would give it a late 12th-century date. In the S aisle windows are pieces of rare 15th-century glass depicting birds. Memorials include cartouches, iron graveslabs and hatchments of the 17th to 19th centuries. Outside are 18th-century chest tombs, carved gravestones and several Harmer terracottas.

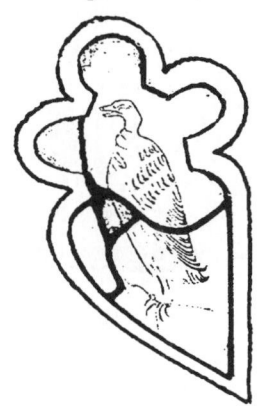

15th-century glass

Seaford *St Leonard*

Seaford was an important Norman harbour and had a substantial church. Its prosperity continued into the 13th century but then declined, the Black Death, the ravages of French raiders and finally the diversion of the sea trade to Newhaven all contributing. Little survives from the Norman church: the western bay of the nave (now part of the lower tower), the N aisle with two tiny round-headed windows and a small carving of St Michael and the Dragon. At the end of the 12th century new nave arcades were built in the Transitional style with low round pillars and responds; one capital (S) is carved with biblical scenes, the rest with stiff-leaf foliage. In the 13th century Early English lancets were added to the clerestory. Late in the 15th century the W

St Michael

tower was built within the Norman nave, the two lower stages being encased by the Norman walls. The upper stages are Perpendicular, built of green sandstone and decorated with alternating panels of stone and knapped flint. The tower, with battlements and a tiled Sussex cap, dominates views of the town. In the 19th-century restoration, the nave was lengthened by a further bay and a new chancel, transepts and polygonal apse were constructed.

Sedlescombe *St John the Baptist* 71E

The oldest part of the church is the N wall, thought to date from the 13th century. There were major changes in the 15th century when the W tower and a new N arcade were built and Perpendicular windows inserted.

Font cover

The 19th-century restoration produced an extension of the nave, a new chancel and the addition of a S aisle, porch and vestry. The crown-post roof with moulded tie-beams and wall plates is mainly of the 15th century; the old beam dated 1632 was part of a gallery re-used when the nave was enlarged. Of early 16th-century date are the font and its cover with linenfold panelling and folding doors. In the N aisle is an iron graveslab with crude lettering; a window contains 16th-century armorial stained glass. From the 17th century are Jacobean carved panels re-used in the pews and, mounted above the S door, a funeral helm with the Sackville crest. A 17th-century church plan shows the allotment of seats to families of the parish.

Selham St James

This building shows the problem of dating precisely an 11th-century church in Sussex from architectural evidence. Herringbone work in the chancel wall is characteristic of the early Norman period. The N door (high, narrow and with simple round arch) has both Saxon and Norman features. The chancel arch is exceptional, quite unlike any other in Sussex. The round arch is Norman but the elaborately decorated capitals and abaci are a mixture of Saxon interlace and intertwined snakes and Norman moulding and foliage. The building belongs to the Saxo-Norman overlap. In addition to the 11th-century nave and chancel, there was a S chapel of the 13th century which was rebuilt in the 19th. The W wall and bellcote are also 19th-century. A large tub font (c.1100) sits on a hexagonal base.

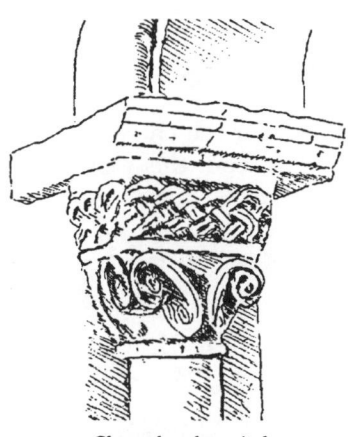

Chancel arch capital

Selmeston

Paintings in the nave show the church as it appeared before 1867 when it was largely rebuilt. Little is left of the earlier building though the present church follows the previous plan and most of the windows are copies of the originals. Medieval details remaining are the W doorway, a holy water stoup in the porch and, in the chancel, a 13th-century piscina and a Perpendicular Easter Sepulchre. Set in the floor of the S aisle is a brass to Henry Rogers (d.1639), 'a painefull Preacher in this church two and thirty yeeres'. Of particular interest is the unusual wooden arcade separating the nave and S aisle. This has two octagonal pillars, 14th-century in style, which support arches of curved braces. Part of a 13th-century font was found

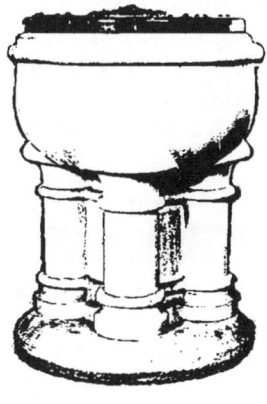

Font

when the lychgate was rebuilt; the 19th-century font now in use is probably a replica of the old one. The circular churchyard, one of a few in Sussex, is a possible indication of Saxon age. Selmeston is an ancient place, having been occupied since the Mesolithic period.

Selsey *St Wilfrid* 89W

Except for the chancel, the church at Church Norton was demolished in 1864 and the materials were used in building Selsey's present church of St Peter a mile to the south. The old chancel, now a chapel dedicated to St Wilfrid and in the care of the Redundant Churches Fund, still stands on the wild shore of Pagham harbour. It is a simple 13th-century structure with clasping buttresses at the E end and lancets in N and S walls. There is a later Perpendicular E window. Inside are two arched recesses (S), one now a credence, the other a piscina. Set in the floor are tapering graveslabs of the 13th/14th centuries, some with raised crosses. A 16th-century tomb recess of Caen stone in the N wall commemorates a Lord of the Manor and his wife; beside their kneeling figures are depicted St George and the martyrdom of St Agatha. One window contains modern stained glass showing the flora and fauna of Pagham harbour. Enough is left of the chancel arch, now bricked in to form the W wall, to see that it was late 12th-century. The original Transitional nave arcades were re-erected in St Peter's. The Norman font from the old church is also there.

16th-century memorial (detail)

Shermanbury *St Giles* 21

Shermanbury is a mile north of Henfield; the church stands along a farm road, beside Shermanbury Place and near medieval Ewhurst Manor. St Giles' has a small aisleless nave, short chancel, a weatherboarded bell turret and W porch. A chapel was recorded here in the Domesday Survey; the 12th-century corbel heads reset in the interior

W wall are possibly from this building. The present nave is of the 13th century; in the nave S wall is a piscina of that period and, to the west, an old carved tie-beam that may have marked the original position of the chancel. The font is of similar age, octagonal with quatrefoils and trefoil arches. There are remains of medieval N and S doorways but most of the stonework is hidden by rendering. The church was restored c.1710 (the carved framework around the chancel entrance dates from that time, as do the windows and the Royal Arms of Queen Anne) and again in the 19th century. The present interior is very much the product of these restorations: a wooden organ gallery to the west, box pews painted with the names of the parish farms, wood and brass candle holders, the ornate woodwork of chancel and choir stalls.

Carved font

Shipley *St Mary* 12

Shipley lies on a narrow Wealden lane near Horsham. The approach by footpath across the river Adur gives the finest view of its impressive early Norman church, built by the Knights Templars in the 12th century. A massive central tower stands between a long nave and short chancel. The nave S doorway has Saxon proportions and the original windows are double splayed, a rare feature in post-Conquest building. The W doorway has zig-zag decoration, jamb shafts and finely carved capitals. The S porch is 16th-century; a 14th-century timber N porch is now a tool shed in the churchyard. Before the Victorian N aisle and vestry were added, the interior was a long rectangle. The

Tower arch corbel

imposing tower arches have roll moulding with a design of chevron and triangular shapes reminiscent of beakheads. Below the W arch the soffit is approximately 2.5 m thick; the corbels are carved with grinning masks. In the chancel are a piscina, sedile and two aumbries. A 17th-century alabaster monument to Sir Thomas Caryll and his wife has life-sized recumbent figures with kneeling daughters and a baby below. The Shipley reliquary, a rare treasure made by the enamellers of Limoges in the 13th century, was stolen in 1976; a card replica stands in its place.

Shoreham   See **New Shoreham** and **Old Shoreham**.

Sidlesham *St Mary* 89W

Sidlesham, near Pagham Harbour, has a large Early English church consisting of aisled nave, crossing and N and S transepts; the 13th-century church also had transept E aisles and chancel which were later demolished. The battlemented tower is probably 16th-century. An 18th-century brick porch leads to a light and lofty interior. The three-bay arcades with round pillars and pointed arches give onto narrow aisles. Two 19th-century dormer windows in the S aisle are fitted with clear glass as are all others in the church. The E window in the present chancel (formerly the crossing) has three trefoil-headed lights with Perpendicular tracery. In the transepts are pairs of tall lancets; the remains of arches which led to the former aisles can be seen in the E walls. Both the brass chandelier and the iron screen date from the 18th century. The 13th-century square font has carved decoration similar to that at Pagham. It rests on a central stem with corner shafts and stands on a platform part of which is a medieval graveslab. Memorials include a monument with kneeling figures to George Taylor and his wife (d.1631) and the earliest surviving graveboard in Sussex (1658) now preserved in the S aisle.

Font

Singleton *The Blessed Virgin Mary* 81W

Singleton, north of Chichester, has one of the county's notable Saxon churches. Its pre-Conquest tower and high nave walls are of flint, plastered, with limestone dressings. The stone is unusual, a pumice-like material from the Isle of Wight found in other Saxon churches in Sussex. In the lowest stage of the tower are three small double-splayed windows. Within the church in the E wall of the tower is a large opening with gabled head, level with the top of the nave walls. This may have led into a chamber above the nave used as accommodation for the priests of the Hundred of Singleton. The S arcade is 13th-century. The N arcade, in similar Early English style, was probably built during a renovation of the church in the 15th century; also

Rood loft stairway

of this date is a well preserved rood loft stair. Many pews have Tudor woodwork. During the 16th century the three-light windows in the late Perpendicular style were added and the tombs of two Earls of Chichester were placed in the sanctuary. In the S aisle is an 18th-century marble tablet to a Huntsman of the once-famous Charlton Hunt; his epitaph ends 'Unpleasing Truth - Death hunts us from our Birth/ In view; and Men, like Foxes, take to Earth'.

Slaugham *St Mary*   22

Slaugham is a parish of four scattered communities in the north of the county divided by the A23. A blocked N doorway shows the Norman origins of the church. The tower, arcades and chancel are from c.1290; the E window is Decorated with three lights and cusped quatrefoils above. In 1613 the Covert chapel was built to the south of the chancel. In the 19th century a small S aisle was replaced by one as wide as the chapel so that the church is now rectangular with the nave and chancel arcades down the middle. The font is typically Norman, a square bowl on a central column with supporting corner shafts; unique in Sussex is the decoration, one side having a carving of a fish. Several monuments are to the Covert family. The earliest is a large brass of 1503 to Sir John,

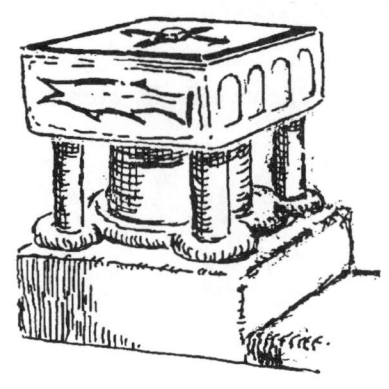

Norman font

a figure under a canopy. On the N side of the chancel and for use as an Easter Sepulchre is a canopied tomb chest of 1547; brasses depicting Sir Richard and his three wives are inset in the wall. The finest is a large stone monument of 1579 on the chapel wall to a later Sir Richard. Elaborately carved, it has a line of seventeen kneeling figures: Sir Richard, his wives and children. In the churchyard are wooden graveboards and 18th-century gravestones.

Slindon St Mary   90W

Slindon lies in the rolling wooded country west of Arundel. The church is of flint rubble with a variety of stone dressings under tiled roofs. The oldest part is the nave and in the N wall is a small early 12th-century window. The most interesting architectural features are the three-bay arcades to N and S aisles. The two E bays (S) are Transitional, their pointed arches resting on rectangular piers (parts of the old nave wall) with semi-circular responds and scalloped capitals.

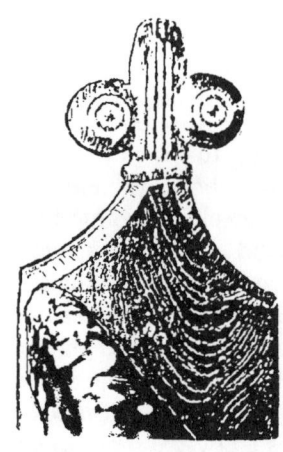

Bench end

The E bay of the N arcade originally led to a transeptal chapel; corbels supporting the arch are typical of the 13th century and similar to those at Climping and Oving. The other arches date from c.1400 when the rest of the N aisle was built and the nave was extended westwards. Although the construction of a tower was begun soon afterwards, the present tower is mainly 16th-century. The chancel is Early English. The font can be dated to the 13th century by its moulded shafts. Ancient woodwork includes the N door, benches with crude poppy-heads and, unique in Sussex, an oak effigy of a knight (Sir Anthony St Leger, d.1539).

Sompting *St Mary*  10

Sompting is famous for its tower with a four-sided gabled spire (unique in this country) known from continental examples as a 'Rhenish helm'. Long considered to be wholly Saxon, it is now believed that only the lower part is Saxon and that the upper parts date from the end of the 11th century and later. It exhibits many of the characteristic features of Saxon buildings such as pilaster strips, long and short work and windows with gabled heads. The tower arch to the nave is 11th-century, its capitals decorated with foliage and scroll patterns. In the late 12th century the church was given to the Knights Templars who rebuilt the nave and chancel, possibly on earlier foundations. They added a large N transept with a stone vaulted E aisle to contain two chapels. The central arches of the vault rest on a corbel in the shape of a large

Tower with Rhenish helm

head. To the south they built a transeptal chapel for their own use; this now forms the church entrance and baptistery, the latter containing a circular Norman font of Sussex marble. Most windows are 15th-century and the S porch, enclosing a Norman doorway, is probably 16th-century. There are many small details of note: re-used Roman bricks in the tower, pieces of Saxon carving in the piscina, ancient sculpture reset in the walls.

South Bersted *St Mary Magdalene* 90W

The seaside resort of Bognor grew out of the village of South Bersted which is now engulfed by modern houses and busy roads; a few flint walls and cottages remain. St Mary's is a large Early English church of the 13th century. The W tower, with shingled spire, is mainly of this date; the massive buttresses are believed to date from the 16th-century 'reparations to the steeple'. The N aisle windows are in the Decorated style and one at least is ancient; a S aisle window (16th-century) has grotesque heads as label stops. Old photographs show that the chancel was demolished in the restoration of 1879 but some lancet windows have been re-used. The N porch, chapel and vestry are modern. Inside are 13th-century five-bay arcades with alternate round and octagonal pillars; the arches are supported at the responds by fluted corbels similar to other churches nearby (Climping and Oving). The string course and piscina in the chancel are from the original church. Old woodwork includes a 13th-century parish chest with carved roundels and the 15th century village pillory in the tower. On the S wall are the arms of the See of Canterbury (the Archbishop has the gift of the living) and the Royal Arms of the Hanoverian kings.

13th-century chest

Southease

There has been a church at Southease for over a thousand years; the British Museum has a Charter issued by King Edgar in 966 granting the church and manor to Hyde Abbey in Winchester. The present church dates from the early 12th century; a notable feature is its round tower, one of three in Sussex, all in the Ouse valley. A former chancel and aisles have gone; the present chancel was originally part of the nave. There are two Norman windows in the tower, others in the nave (S wall) and one (blocked) high on the N wall. The chancel, entered through a modern wooden arch, has a three-light 14th-century E window. The communion rail is Jacobean and there are 17th-century seats and memorial slabs. Medieval wall paintings, discovered this century, depict scenes from the life of Christ and once covered the entire church. The church has two bells, one of which dates from c.1280. The mahogany cased organ with gilded pipes is a fine and rare example of 18th-century craftsmanship.

Round tower

South Harting *St Mary & St Gabriel* 71W

The large cruciform church at South Harting has a dominant position above the village street; a broach spire, covered with copper in the 18th century, rises from the tower. Most of the building dates from c.1300 but extensive reconstruction followed a serious fire in 1576. On the S side are the ruins of the 17th-century Caryll mortuary chapel. In the high, narrow nave are three-bay arcades to N and S aisles. New tower arches were built after the fire and above one (E) can be seen part of the original arch with dogtooth moulding; near the S arch is a rood loft piscina. Decorated three-light windows have a variety of tracery including Geometrical (N transept), intersecting (chancel) and cusped Y-tracery (S transept). In the S transept are also three 17th-century effigies rearranged from the original monument. A weathered effigy of Sir Richard Caryll (d.1616) was transferred from the ruined chapel. The Elizabethan chancel roof has tie-beams with pendants, ornamented wall-posts and balusters to collar beams. The oak spiral staircase to the tower was designed and constructed in 1848 by a local craftsman. The 13th-century Purbeck marble font, square with carved arcading, has a Jacobean cover.

Spiral staircase

South Malling *St Michael* 41

The Domesday Book records that 'the canons of St Michael's hold 4 hides', evidence of a religious community at Malling in the 11th century. The present church dates from 1626 when John Evelyn, then a schoolboy at Lewes, laid the foundation stone, his father having been instrumental in the building of St Michael's. It consists of a nave and chancel in one space and a low W tower with a pyramidal roof; on the S porch is the completion date, 1628. The N vestries are modern. Older features in the church are reset from the ruins of the collegiate church at Malling: two small capitals with stiff-leaf foliage (E wall), the 14th-century tower arch and Decorated E window. In 1874 the classical windows were replaced by the present pointed ones. There are two small brasses on the N wall. A black and white memorial is to those killed in the winter of 1836 when an avalanche destroyed a workhouse below the hill at Cliffe.

Porch doorway

South Stoke *St Leonard* 01

The quiet hamlet of South Stoke lies in a loop of the river Arun; although only two miles from Arundel it sees few visitors. A community and church here were recorded in the Domesday Survey. The church is essentially the original 11th-century building with additional 13th-century work. Norman details remaining are the N and S doorways; the one on the north is blocked. The 13th-century entrance porch has a vaulted roof with chamfered ribs. There was extensive restoration in the 19th century when the chateau-like spire was added to the slender tower. Inside, the tower is open to the belfry stage; an impressive feature is the arch to the nave, tall, narrow and double-chamfered. The nave is wide, unaisled, with lancet windows and a crown-post roof. The chancel arch is of clunch, a hard building chalk; it dates from the restoration, as does the E window. The church is illuminated by candles set in rods behind the pews.

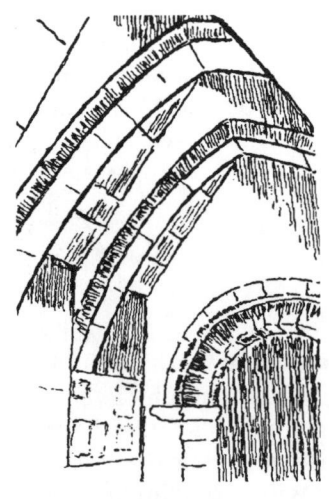
Vaulted porch

Southwick *St Michael & All Angels*

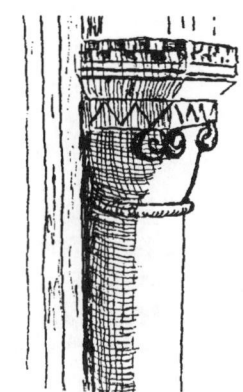
Shaft decoration

As a result of bomb damage in 1941, the church tower had to be taken down; it was reconstructed in 1951 from the carefully numbered stones and timbers. The lower stages are of the 11th or 12th centuries (see the arch and shaft decoration and the small windows), the upper stage Transitional with pointed arches. The nave and aisles are Victorian, rebuilt after a fire. A notable feature of the chancel is the round-headed Norman S arcade uncovered in the 19th century. The carving on the capitals (billet and volutes) recurs in the ground stage of the tower. From the 13th century are the chancel arch, N wall lancets and the square font. The 14th-century rood screen has been re-positioned across the S aisle. The pulpit has Jacobean carved panels. At the W end are the carved Royal Arms of the late Hanoverian period.

Stedham *St James*

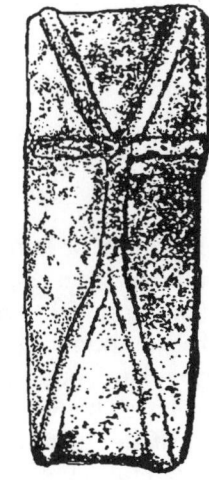
Graveslab

A church at Stedham was recorded in the Domesday Book but the present building of local sandstone is of the 17th and 19th centuries. Old carved stones from an early church are incorporated in the nave S wall and below it, near the porch, are ancient headstones and graveslabs, 11th or 12th-century. The earlier part is the tower of 1673; a two-light square-headed window has the date above. The tower, now used as a vestry, is finished with a parapet and a low octagonal spire. The cup-shaped font is possibly 12th-century. A 13th-century chest is carved with roundels and has the remains of several old locks. An extremely large yew in the churchyard has a trunk of over 8m in girth and is almost certainly older than the church.

Steyning *St Andrew*

The Saxon church at Steyning, founded by St Cuthman, was replaced in the 12th century by a large Norman cruciform church of which the aisled and clerestoried nave remains. The chancel was rebuilt in the 18th century and again in 1863. After the central tower was removed in the 16th century, the chequered stone and flint tower was built at the W end. The 15th-century S entrance porch encloses a Norman doorway with decorated mouldings. There is then a descent to the magnificent late Norman nave, possibly the finest of this period in the country. Four-bay arcades of Caen stone have large round pillars on massive square bases. Capitals and arches are richly ornamented, each with a different motif; decorated labels over the arches have grotesque head-stops. A string course runs below the shafted clerestory windows. Of the former crossing arches the sole survivor is the superb chancel arch. This and the flanking aisle arches date from c.1100 and are the oldest remaining features. An early 12th-century capital (S aisle) has two lions with a single head; a lower panel depicts men enmeshed in tendrils. The square Norman font, carved with a V-shaped pattern, is of Purbeck marble. On the W wall are the Royal Arms of Queen Anne (1703). The finely carved oak panelling behind the altar, dated 1522, was originally in the vicarage.

Norman capital

Stopham *St Mary*

Stopham is best known for its medieval stone bridge over the Arun. Even older is the church which has a nave and chancel built soon after the Conquest. The early date is apparent on the outside from the tiny blocked window in the chancel N wall, the decoration of the S doorway and, on the inside, the high, narrow doorways. The Norman chancel arch has quarter-round moulding on its E face; to the north is a recess of the late 12th century. An arch over the sanctuary suggests that originally the chancel had an apsidal end. There are windows in the Early English and Decorated styles. The three-light E window is

17th-century, filled with contemporary armorial glass. Of the same age is the glass with kneeling figures in the nave N wall. Members of the Barttelot family, Lords of the Manor for centuries, are commemorated in brasses set in the Sussex marble floor: four double brasses in the nave, a triple brass in the chancel, all with attendant figures of children and coats of arms. The Perpendicular octagonal font has quatrefoil carving on the bowl. The W tower, rebuilt c.1600, retains old wooden shutters at the belfry windows.

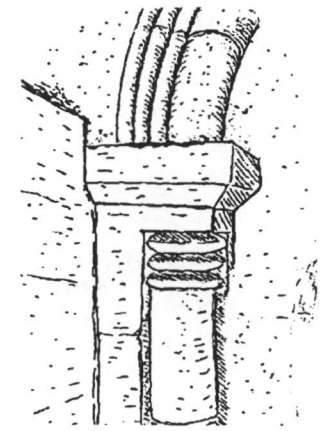

South doorway (detail)

Storrington *St Mary* 01

Over many centuries Storrington has grown from village to small town and in that time St Mary's has grown from a simple 11th-century church into a large building with aisled nave, chancel with chapels and a W tower. The N aisle and chapel comprise the Domesday Book church of nave and chancel, although little recognisable remains apart from the high walls, the blocked N doorway and the jambs and imposts of the original chancel arch. At some stage the Norman church was given a S aisle which in time became the nave of the church, as it still is today. A chancel was built to the east in the 13th century. The medieval tower collapsed in the 18th century bringing down part of the nave; it was rebuilt c.1750. In the 19th century the chancel was extended and the present S aisle added, its arcade a copy of the N arcade. The nave, with its pillars of attached octagonal shafts, is therefore of several dates though of uniform Perpendicular style. In the sanctuary is a wall-mounted brass of 1591 commemorating a former rector. There are 18th-century charity boards in the tower.

Nave pillar

Stoughton *St Mary* 81W

Stoughton is in the wooded Downs NW of Chichester near the site of a famous Saxon battle. St Mary's has Saxon features (very tall, thin walls, double splayed windows, transeptal chapels) but most of the church is Norman, late 11th and 12th-century. It consists of chancel, nave, transepts (with a tower built over southern one) and a 17th-century brick S porch. The walls are mainly plastered and, where some has fallen off the tower, herringbone flintwork can be seen. The oldest windows, double-splayed, are in the transept W walls. A single, large, round-headed light forms the chancel E window; in the N and S walls are similar windows, beheaded when the chancel roof was lowered. The interior is impressive for the cliff-like walls (over 10m tall) and the majestic chancel arch of two orders with roll mouldings on the soffit and jambs, similar in design and age to that at Bosham. There is evidence of some rebuilding in the 13th century (the transept arches are pointed but on older jambs). The tower, supported inside the church on a massive wooden framework, dates from the 14th century. There are 13th-century piscinae in both transepts; that in the north has heads as label stops and is surrounded with dogtooth ornament. The font is thought to be a modern copy of a Norman design.

Piscina

Streat 31

Wall tablet (detail)

The church is situated on a Roman road, 'The Greensand Way', with a wide view to the north slope of the Downs. Heavily restored in the 19th century, the oldest part is the Norman nave but all original details have gone — Hussey in 1852 wrote of N and S round-headed doorways. The chancel was probably rebuilt in the 13th century; the vestry and S aisle are modern. A shingled W bell turret has a steep pyramidal roof. Inside are interesting monuments: elegant and ornate 18th-century wall tablets with cherubs beneath and, on the nave floor, two cast iron memorial slabs. One of these, with several dates of the 18th century, measures approximately 2m by 1m and is the largest in the country. The weight of the slab, made at Lamberhurst in Kent and transported to Streat, must be at least 500 kg. Above the chancel arch are the Royal Arms of Charles II, dated 1660.

Sullington 01

Sullington Lane, a cul-de-sac towards the Downs near Storrington, ends at the beautiful and secluded place where the church, a farm and an ancient tithe barn are situated. The original church was pre-Conquest; the high narrow nave is a distinctive Saxon feature as is the long and short work of the quoins (NW and SW) of the lower tower (the upper stage is 12th-century). Entrance is through the W doorway into the tower, leading to a nave of almost the same width. Tower and chancel arches are early 13th-century. The two-bay arcade gives onto a N aisle, once used as a chantry. The chancel has a 14th-century E window with reticulated tracery. There is a triangular headed aumbry in the N wall; on the S side are a piscina and recessed sedilia. A squint through the S pier of the chancel arch was possibly connected with an anchorite's cell outside the church; a low side lancet window nearby contains 15th-century Belgian glass. Displayed at the W end of the nave is a large 15th-century stone coffin slab. The Perpendicular font has carved quatrefoils. A 13th-century effigy of a knight in chain mail is badly mutilated but notable for its early date and excellent detail.

Long and short work

Sutton St John   91W

The scarp slope of the Downs south of Petworth changes direction for a mile or so from East-West to North-South. In the corner thus created, under a high wooded part of the Downs, lies Sutton. The church, large

Tomb recess

for such a village, has a late 12th-century nave and S arcade with round pillars, waterleaf capitals and Transitional pointed arches; the S aisle was mainly rebuilt in the 19th century. The W tower of c.1300 has trefoil-headed belfry openings and high interior arch. From the 14th-century Decorated period are the chancel arch and chancel with triple sedilia and a piscina in the S wall. There is a shallow N transept, also Decorated. In the nave (N wall) is a 15th-century Perpendicular window of three cinquefoil lights under a square head. The 13th-century marble font is octagonal and carved with pointed arches; the bowl stands on a plain central stem surrounded by eight marble shafts. A large recess in the exterior S wall once accommodated an 18th-century tomb. Herringbone masonry in the N wall provides evidence of an earlier church of the 11th century.

Tangmere *St Andrew* 90W

Inhabited in Saxon times, Tangmere village and its church were recorded in the Domesday Survey. The present flint church is early 12th-century and was originally a nave and small chancel; the chancel was extended eastwards in the 13th century. The W bell turret, supported by a framework of heavy oak timbers inside the nave, has a slender spire. A porch (floored with old tapering graveslabs) and a tiny vestry annexe at the W end are modern additions. High in the N and S nave walls are small Norman windows, two on each side; the stone at the head of one (S) is a carving, possibly Saxon, thought to represent the beheading of John the Baptist. In the nave, which has a roof with old tie-beams, is the plain tub-shaped font, one of the oldest in Sussex. The chancel arch and windows are 13th-century with two large, elegant lancets in the E wall; on the S side is a trefoil-headed

Saxon carving

piscina. In the churchyard is a hollow yew tree which may be even older than the church. A moving reminder of more recent times are the graves of young airmen, British, Allied and German, who died at Tangmere RAF Station in the second world war.

Tarring Neville *St Mary*  40

'Tarring' indicates the early Saxon origin of this small community on the lower Ouse, 'Neville' its medieval Lords of the Manor. The church is of flint and sandstone with rendered walls and tiled roofs. It has a Norman Transitional nave and S aisle and an Early English W tower and chancel. Inside, the two-bay arcade has a round pillar and capital and double-chamfered arches. The Early English chancel arch, somewhat mis-shapen, has needed concrete reinforcement. The chancel is almost as long as the nave and has, in N and S walls, both single and twin lancets under scoinson arches. The triple-lancet E window is modern. The 14th-century octagonal font was built into the S wall in the 19th century. An immense 18th-century black marble memorial slab before the altar is to a former incumbent. In the aisle is an old iron chest reputed to be from a ship of the Armada.

Twin lancets

Telscombe *St Laurence*  40

Telscombe shelters in a wooded Downland hollow. Its church of flint and sandstone is set on a steep bank in the centre of the village. It has a Norman nave, N aisle and chancel of the early 12th century. The tower and N chapel were added later in the same century. Inside, the nave arcade has round pillars and abaci supporting plain round arches. There are two 15th-century Perpendicular windows in the nave S wall. The chancel arch is Victorian. In the chancel are two 13th-century lancet windows; the E window, of simple Decorated design, and the small piscina both date from the 14th century. The most elaborate

Sussex cap

stonework is in the N chapel arcade which has a round pillar with square abacus and corner corbels decorated with stiff-leaf foliage. A modern window in the chapel is filled with a mosaic of ancient coloured glass. The Stuart Royal Arms, carved in high relief, are above the door. The medieval square font of green sandstone is carved on each side with lancets and set on a base with deeply cut trefoil-headed arches.

Terwick St Peter 82W

Terwick church stands by itself in fields, half a mile east of Rogate. A small 12th century building of stone rubble, it consists of chancel and nave with bellcote. At the W end are modern vestries and a porch. A blocked opening in the S wall has the appearance of a former priest's doorway but was actually a low side window which was later extended to ground level. The two lancets on either side are 13th-century (restored); other lancets, including those in the E wall are modern. Above the W doorway, with tall inner arch, is a small 12th-century window, round-headed and deeply splayed. The ancient W door has been replaced but its old hinges are fitted to the new door. There is a single old tie-beam in the nave roof. Two 15th-century windows have cinquefoil-headed lights, three (N) under a four-centred arch and two (S) under a square head. The chancel arch is modern. There is a 17th-century communion rail. The 12th-century font is tub-shaped and rests on a cylindrical stem. In the churchyard opposite the W door is a curious old cross of uncertain date.

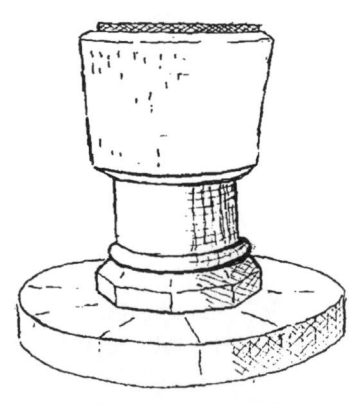

Norman font

Thakeham *St Mary*

Thakeham is a small village but its church is large and imposing. The nave, chancel and transepts date from the 12th and 13th centuries and are of local sandstone and ironstone under Horsham slab roofs. From the 16th century are the S porch (with original timbers) and tower, with angle buttresses, battlements and an uncommon ridged roof. The 12th-century nave has a single Norman window in the N wall. The chancel arch and parts of the N transept are Transitional; it is believed that the transept was formerly a N tower. The chancel and transepts have Early English lancet windows in deeply splayed openings. Much woodwork dates from about 1500: the small door to the tower stairs, the screen across the tower arch (possibly the former rood) and the pews with Tudor rose decoration. The 15th-century font is octagonal and ornately carved. There are memorials to the Apsley family of nearby Thakeham Place: two small figure brasses on the nave floor, a wall monument in classical style (N transept) and three tomb chests in the chancel, all of the 16th century. One tomb is covered with an alabaster slab engraved with the effigy of a man in armour, the lines filled with pitch to emphasise the figure.

Tudor bench end

Ticehurst *St Mary*

The large sandstone church at Ticehurst, a hill-top village near the Kent border, was built mainly in the 14th century when the Sussex iron industry flourished in the area. Its W tower has a NE stair turret and is surmounted by a shingled spire; above the moulded W doorway is a large four-light Perpendicular window with original tracery. The two-storeyed N porch has quadripartite vaulting with the Etchingham arms on the central boss. Inside are four-bay arcades to N and S aisles and two-bay arcades to the chapels. An impressive feature is the tall tower arch; the windows and walls each side remain from the 13th-century building. From the 19th century are the clerestory windows, the chancel arch and the E window. Remains of early 15th-century glass, reset in the sanctuary N window, show part of a Doom with figures in a cauldron (one wearing a crown and another a bishop's mitre) and others in a cart drawn by devils. Also medieval are the doorway of a former rood loft (N), a squint (S wall) and three piscinae (chancel and chapels). Preserved in the church are 18th-century prayer boards, beautifully scripted, and a Victorian bier. The font has a 16th-century octagonal oak cover with folding doors, elaborately carved, similar to those at Rotherfield and Sedlescombe.

15th-century glass

Tillington *All Hallows* 92W

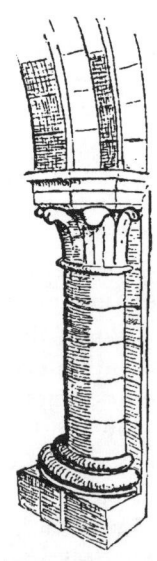

Arcade respond

The present church is largely the result of rebuilding by Lord Egremont of Petworth House in the early 19th century. (Petworth Park adjoins the churchyard.) In 1807 a new S tower was raised and finished with open stonework, known as a Scots Crown. Subsequently a N aisle was added to the nave, the chancel was lengthened and an organ chamber and a W porch of two storeys were built. Masonry in the S wall is the only ancient work visible on the exterior; inside there is more of antiquity. The S arcade of three bays with Transitional pointed arches has a W respond with a scalloped capital. The pillars are round with moulded bases and octagonal abaci and there is a matching E respond. Their capitals have distinctive strap-like leaves as decoration. All this dates from the late 12th century; the N arcade is a 19th-century copy. The chancel arch is 13th-century, as is some of the masonry in the lower stage of the tower. Massive slabs of Sussex marble cover the chancel floor. On the S aisle wall are inscribed memorial brasses dating from the 16th to 20th centuries.

Tortington *St Mary Magdalene* 00

This 12th-century church was built to serve a community of Austin canons whose priory was nearby. Today it stands almost hidden among farm buildings, its white painted bell turret showing above the trees. The church is mainly Norman with flint and rubble walls and quoins of Caen stone. The clay tiled roof, dating from the Victorian restoration, has a 'cat slide' over nave and S aisle. A richly moulded S doorway is decorated with zig-zag ornament, grapes and a star pattern. The windows are round-headed with deep splays. Inside, the Norman chancel arch of Caen stone is of two orders, the inner one plain and the outer having axe-cut

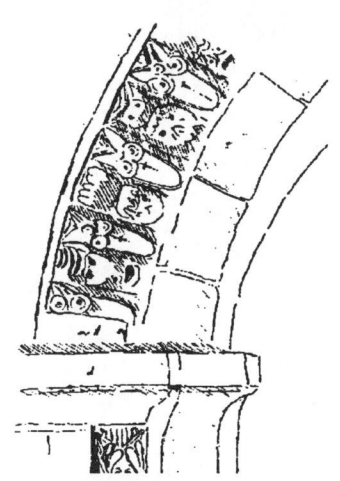

Beakhead decoration

beakheads alternating with grotesque faces. Apart from New Shoreham and Broadwater, there is no other beakhead decoration in Sussex. From the same period and also of Caen stone is the large bowl-shaped font carved with arcading and columns. Formal flower and shell motifs alternate below the arches and the rim has decorative cable moulding. In the S aisle is a 15th-century oak pew with carved panels. The 17th-century pulpit was possibly made locally. Over the chancel arch are two 18th-century hatchments. Since 1987 the church has been in the care of the Redundant Churches Fund.

Trotton *St George* 82W

Trotton, on the western Rother, has a large early 14th-century church, barnlike with undivided nave and chancel of the same width. There is

Brass effigy, c.1310

a W tower with shingled octagonal cap. The nave and chancel have a fine set of windows, four each side, of the Geometrical style, two trefoil-headed lights with a quatrefoil above. Inside, the W wall is covered with painting contemporary with the building depicting, among other things, the Seven Deadly Sins and the Seven Acts of Mercy. Further paintings decorate N and S walls. The roof is original and has curved braces to collar beams and purlins. In the aisle is a magnificent memorial brass to Margaret de Camoys (date c.1310). Recent scholarship considers this to be the earliest full length figure brass in the country. On a tomb chest before the altar and on a massive Purbeck marble slab is a large brass of about 1420, two figures under canopies. This commemorates Thomas, Lord Camoys, (a commander at Agincourt), and his wife (widow of Hotspur and hence the 'Gentle Kate' of Shakespeare's Henry IV).

Twineham *St Peter* 22

Twineham church stands alone at the end of a lane; it dates from the early 16th century when few new churches were built and is entirely of brick. The nave, chancel and tower are all in the Tudor style of architecture; windows and door openings have four-centred arches

West doorway

typical of the period. The tower, whose W door retains the original 16th-century ironwork, is finished with a shingled broach spire. Entrance is through a timber S porch where 17th-century gravestones, formerly in the churchyard, are preserved. The church has Jacobean furnishings including the communion rail and pulpit, an elaborately carved box pew and a font cover (the font itself is 13th-century). A fragment of 15th-century glass (SE nave window) shows the Arms of the de la Warr family. Above the low chancel arch hangs a copy of Procaccini's painting of The Holy Family. The modern reredos incorporates ancient carved panels, probably of the 14th century. An unusual feature in the churchyard is a Quaker burial ground marked by four stones, a plot acquired in 1694 when the then Rector's daughter was married to a Quaker. Although there have been no burials since 1732, a nominal rent is still paid by the Society of Friends.

Uckfield *Holy Cross* 42

A watercolour in the Sharpe collection shows Uckfield church as it was at the end of the 18th century: nave, chancel and 14th-century W tower. Only the tower and part of the chancel wall were retained when the church was rebuilt (and rededicated) in 1839. A nave with aisles and a new chancel were constructed, the tower raised and a shingled spire added. Further additions of organ chamber and chapel were made 50 years later. Inside, the arcades are of three bays with tall plain pillars and four-centred arches. Galleries extend round three sides of the nave; the one on the north carries the date 1720. A few memorials survive from the old church: a brass of 1610 with a coat of arms, figure and inscription, a cast iron graveslab of 1707 and an 18th-century cartouche.

Cartouche

Udimore *St Mary* 81E

The Domesday Survey records a church at Udimore, near Rye, a parish mainly of scattered farmhouses. The oldest part of the present building is the Norman nave which retains one window (blocked) high in the N wall. Arches of a demolished S aisle can be seen in the exterior wall. The chancel and low tower were built c.1230. Incorporated in the modern porch are a 15th-century doorway and small window. Inside, the blocked aisle arcade is still evident. Originally of two bays, it was lengthened by a third (W) built slightly later. There is stiff-leaf carving

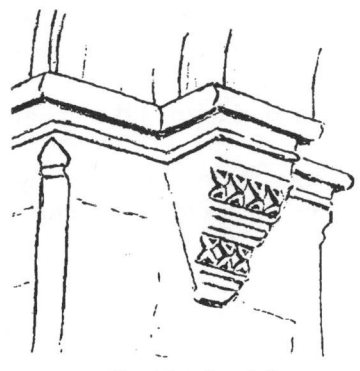

Chancel arch corbel

on the arcade capitals and dogtooth ornament on the corbels of the chancel arch. The Early English chancel remains almost as when built and is an admirable example of the period. A string course runs beneath tall, widely spaced lancet windows, three in each wall; in the S wall are a piscina, a priest's doorway and a former low side window now with the lower part blocked. Several inscribed brasses are set in the floor of the nave and chancel. On a large board are the Royal Arms of George III, dated 1772. The modern font replaces a rare wooden font which stands in the porch.

Up Marden *St Michael* 71W

St Michael's church stands high on the Downs, remote and unrestored, in a churchyard set with yews. Nave, chancel and tower are all 13th-century, as are the single lancet windows. The interior is described in Pevsner as 'one of the loveliest in England'. The unaisled nave has a brick floor, plastered walls and tie-beams painted white or cream. There are two chancel arches because the Early English arch needed emergency repair in the 16th century and so the second, straight sided arch was built below. It is possible that the stones used in the later arch were brought from the demolished chapel at West Marden. The circular font is probably 12th-century; there is a piscina in the nave in an unusual position. In the chancel are 13th-century wall plates with dogtooth decoration; the trefoil-headed piscina has a credence shelf. The church's three bells were removed from the tower as a safety measure; two are on the floor of the chancel and one is mounted outside by the S porch. The church is illuminated by candles.

Chancel arch

Upper Beeding *St Peter*

In 1075 William de Braose, first Lord of Bramber Rape, founded a small priory at Sele, across the river from his castle. St Peter's was the priory church, the monks using the chancel, the parishioners the nave. On the outside of the 12th-century N wall can be seen shallow Norman buttresses and some walling with square blocks of Caen stone. The tower is probably 13th-century. In the 19th-century restoration the S aisle and porch were added and new windows inserted. The chancel has been rebuilt several times and in the S wall contains Norman masonry, part of an arcade of round-headed arches (possibly from the cloisters) and a reset doorway. The octagonal font of Sussex marble is of late medieval date. A fragment of a 15th-century wooden screen hangs above the door. The churchyard wall contains many carved stones from the priory.

Chancel S wall

Upwaltham *St Mary*

In its Downland setting with neighbouring farm buildings, the small flint church at Upwaltham has an appealing simplicity. Unchanged in plan since it was built in the early 12th century, it has an apsidal chancel, one of only five in Sussex. There is a weatherboarded W bell turret and a modern S porch. The high nave, with a timbered roof of tie-beams and crown-posts, is entered through a 14th-century S doorway. There are no original windows; one of three lights (N wall) is of the 16th century and the two windows in the S and W walls are modern. A wide 13th-century arch divides the nave from the chancel; corbels on the soffit once carried a rood beam. The chancel is lit by four trefoil-headed windows; the earliest are

Piscina

those adjacent to the chancel arch and were built soon after its construction. The windows on either side of the altar date from the 15th century. Built into the sedilia on the south is a piscina fashioned from a 12th-century square capital with volute carving. The 12th-century font is tub-shaped and resembles others in the area. There are 18th-century memorials in the nave floor and several in the churchyard.

Wadhurst St Peter & St Paul 63

Wadhurst, in the High Weald, was the centre of the iron industry that brought prosperity from the medieval period until the 18th century. Its large sandstone church has a Norman W tower (see the lower windows and twin bell-openings) with a 14th-century shingled broach spire, sharply pointed. Most of the church dates from the 14th century and the windows are mainly of the late Decorated style; the distinctive aisle windows are similar to nearby Ticehurst. The S porch, with vaulted roof and room above, was built in the 15th century. The interior is spacious and light; the wide nave has four-bay arcades and 16th-century clerestory windows. The circular, moulded font is probably 13th-century. A feature of the church is the number and variety of memorials. Outside are 18th-century gravestones, two carved with Adam and Eve in the Garden, and on the porch wall is a tablet incorporating Harmer terracottas. The church is notable for its iron graveslabs set in the floor; it has far more (over 30) than any other church in the country. The earliest are decorated with just six shields, initials and dates, later ones with inscriptions and coats of arms, fitting memorials to the ironmasters of the Weald.

Iron graveslab

Walberton St Mary 90W

Walberton is a village of the coastal plain to the west of Arundel, a long street with attractive houses near the church. St Mary's has flint rubble walls under tiled roofs. A single sweep of roof covers both nave and aisles and there is a wooden bell turret and spire at the W end. On the N side is the stone entrance porch, a rare 13th-century example, with trefoil-headed windows recessed into the thick walls. The nave is probably pre-Conquest and during the 12th century the walls were pierced by arches of differing height and width but all in early Norman style. The present aisles are of 13th-century date as is the chancel. A feature of the chancel is the large number of aumbries (possibly to house religious relics). Two are behind the altar, one (N wall) has side chambers and another (S wall) reaches down to floor level. At the W end of the nave is massive timber framework supporting the belfry. A stone coffin of great age was found during 19th-century drainage work. The tub-shaped font may be Saxon or early Norman. Many 18th-century carved gravestones can be seen in the churchyard; one is to Charles Cook, killed by a falling tree, whose death is depicted together with symbols of mortality.

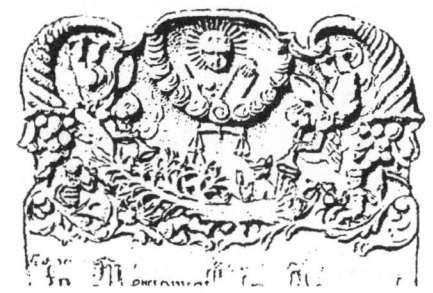

18th-century gravestone

Waldron *All Saints* 51

The Wealden village of Waldron is situated on the edge of a former ironworking area and has a large, mainly Early English church. The chancel, nave, N aisle and W tower date from the 13th century. Later additions to the tower are the stair turret and battlements, the W doorway and window. The S aisle was built in the 19th century. Inside, the four-bay N arcade (octagonal pillars and chamfered arches) is 13th-century, the S arcade a 19th-century copy. The N aisle has some Decorated windows and, at the W end, a lancet with an unusual cusped head. In the chancel are a simple Early

Wooden graveboard

English piscina and an aumbry. A widely splayed lancet (N) contains old glass, the quarries painted with wheat and vine leaves. The pre-Reformation altar slab with incised crosses, now used in the N aisle chapel, was found during the 19th-century restoration. Memorials include 17th-century ledger slabs and inscribed brasses in the floor, 18th-century cartouches on the walls and an elegant marble monument to John Fuller, an ironmaster. Two large hatchments hang in the tower. In the churchyard are Harmer terracottas and several wooden graveboards.

Warbleton *St Mary* 61

Warbleton, six miles north of Hailsham, is on a ridge of the High Weald; from St Mary's churchyard are extensive views to the South Downs. The exterior shows several architectural styles. The Early English chancel has lancets, one of which (S wall) was later altered into a low side window; near it is an unusual tomb recess. The nave and N aisle windows are Decorated. From the Perpendicular period are the tower with large protruding heads at the top, the chancel and chapel E windows and, inside, the four-bay arcade. Prominent in the aisle is the large squire's pew (1722) set high on posts and reached by a staircase; above it are two hatchments. Old glass in three windows includes 15th-century heraldic glass (chancel NE). Near the pulpit is the doorway to a former rood loft. On the chancel floor is a large canopied brass to William Prestwyck (d.1436). A splendid marble monument by Rysbrack, unhappily positioned behind the organ, is to Sir John Lade (d.1740), a bust on a pedestal framed by columns with pediment and backed by finely sculpted floral decoration. Less grand, but also of interest, are two churchyard gravestones with Harmer terracottas.

Squire's pew

Warminghurst *The Holy Sepulchre* 11

A field path from Thakeham leads to Warminghurst church, isolated but for a neighbouring farmhouse. Built in the 13th century, it is small and rectangular with no structural division between nave and chancel. A brick S porch (blocked) and N vestry date from the 17th and 18th centuries. In the W wall, which is mainly of coursed Sussex marble, is a 13th-century roundel. A shingled bell turret houses a bell of c.1200, one of the oldest in Sussex. Tall, deeply splayed lancets and a three-light E window are fitted with clear glass, giving brightness to the lovely interior. The church is furnished with 18th-century pine box pews and a three-decker pulpit.

Pulpit

A wooden arched screen painted with the Royal Arms of Queen Anne makes the division between nave and chancel. The communion rail with close twisted balusters and the oak altar table are 17th-century. A wall brass has figures of Edward Shelley (d.1554) and his wife kneeling with their ten children. There are two large 18th-century memorial tablets and three hatchments. Above the font is a decorative wrought iron bracket with a pulley for raising the cover. After years of neglect the church was sensitively restored in 1959 and is now cared for by the Redundant Churches Fund.

Warnham *St Margaret*

Warnham, near Horsham, has a large sandstone church under Horsham slab roofs. Only the font remains from the Norman church that belonged to nearby Rusper nunnery. From the 14th century are parts of the nave arcades, the N aisle, chancel and most of the N chapel. The S chapel and tower are of 16th-century date. During the 19th century the church was enlarged and the west front, chancel and S aisle were rebuilt. The nave has four-bay arcades with octagonal pillars and moulded capitals; the roof is a modern hammerbeam construction. A large dormer window dates from 1907. The N aisle leads through a screen with 14th-century woodwork

The Caryll memorial (detail)

into the Caryll chapel. This contains a large, alabaster memorial to Sir John Caryll (d.1613) and his wife with kneeling figures; beneath are their children, four bearing skulls denoting early death. In the floor are two fine ledger slabs, one to a member of the Shelley family which had close links with the church. (The poet was christened here.) The 12th-century marble font has a square bowl with shallow arcading. In the S aisle are instruments and music of a 19th-century choirmaster; his gravestone with epitaph in verse is in the churchyard.

Wartling St Mary Magdalene 60

Wartling is on a hill rising from the Pevensey Levels. The spire of Pevensey church, four miles distant, and the tower of neighbouring Westham can be seen in the extensive view south from the churchyard. The church is built of local sandstone. The walls of nave and chancel are probably 13th-century but no detail from that period survives. At the E end of the nave are short aisles and over the W bay is a weatherboarded bell turret with a low spire. The N entrance porch is modern; a brick S porch has the date 1737 over the doorway. Two carved stones set in the S aisle wall depict the Pelham buckle and a Catherine wheel. Inside, the N and S two-bay arcades differ in length and detail, that on the north being earlier. Above the chancel arch are the Royal Arms of George II. The church has box pews and an 18th-century pulpit. A recent addition to the furnishings is the modern lectern which takes the form of a heron carved in elm, appropriate in a parish with several heronries. The wall tablets include a number to the Curteis family with typical Georgian motifs. A Harmer plaque on the nave wall (S) is the only known example cast in iron and was originally one of a pair made for a churchyard graveboard.

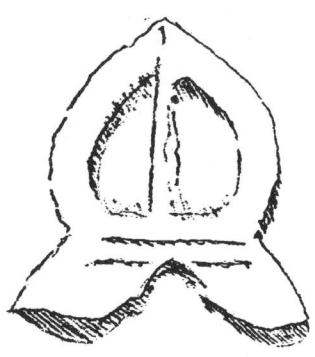

The Pelham buckle

Washington St Mary 11

Washington is at the north end of the gap in the Downs through which runs the Worthing to London road. The church was originally Norman but its early history has been obscured by the rebuilding of the 19th century. Everything was demolished except for the Transitional N arcade and the late Perpendicular W tower, built during the reign of Henry VII. The tower is short and sturdy, surmounted by a tiled Sussex cap enclosed by battlements, and from the west, with a flag flying, looking almost like a small castle. The belfry openings have unusual tracery. The typical Perpendicular font is octagonal with panels of pointed arches having trefoil and cinquefoil heads. A marble wall tablet of 1600 shows mother, father and seven children in the dress of the period.

Tudor tower

West Blatchington *St Peter* 20

Once a remote Downland settlement, West Blatchington is now part of the Brighton conurbation; its church and a neighbouring windmill are surrounded by suburban houses. A photograph taken before the 19th-century rebuilding shows St Peter's roofless and in ruins, the result of neglect from the 17th century onwards. At the restoration the old ruins were incorporated in the new building and most of the S and W walls remain from the original 12th-century church. In the W wall are two narrow Norman windows with a modern triple-light window in the gable above; the change from medieval walling to that of the 19th century is clearly visible externally. An ancient graveslab in the ground in front is apparently still in its original position. By the mid 20th century the church was proving inadequate for a rapidly expanding population and in 1961 a large extension, in effect a new church con-

The church c.1830

sisting of nave and chancel, was built immediately to the north. The two naves are interconnected by a five-bay arcade with a clerestory above. A list of Rectors of West Blatchington dates back to 1307.

Westbourne *St John the Baptist* 70W

Westbourne is a mile north of Emsworth; the nearby river Ems forms the boundary with Hampshire. The large church, of flint with ashlar dressings, consists of nave with aisles and N and S porches, chancel

Nave arcade

with N sacristy and S organ chamber and a battlemented tower with octagonal spire. Although Norman pillar bases have been found under the nave, the oldest visible work is 13th-century walling in the aisles and chancel (note the blocked E lancets). From the late 14th century are the sacristy, the W ends of the aisles and the Perpendicular aisle windows. These are of two lights dividing into four small lights above; the modern copies date from the 19th century. The nave arcades (octagonal pillars and four centred arches) were built in the 16th century. At the same

time the tower, supported on four huge piers, was rebuilt within the body of the church; the spire is 18th-century. Most of the 16th-century N porch has been renewed but it contains an old beam bearing coats of arms. Among the 18th-century gravestones in the churchyard is one commemorating a farmer, carved with a wheatsheaf, scythe and rake.

West Chiltington *St Mary* 01

The church at West Chiltington near Pulborough dates from the 12th century and is largely unrestored. Built of stone rubble, it consists of chancel, nave with S aisle and a 14th-century S chapel; the spire is dated 1602. The large Norman N doorway has zig-zag and roll moulding and is enclosed by a 13th-century porch. Inside are extensive wall paintings, the church's most notable feature and a reminder of the colourful interiors customary in medieval churches. On the nave walls are 13th-century scenes of the Nativity (N) and the Passion (S). In a

window splay is a figure of
Christ whose blood from
wounded hands falls on
tradesmen's tools, a warning
against Sabbath work. The
earliest paintings (12th-century)
around the arch in the S aisle
depict angels and apostles.
There is an exceptionally long
squint (about 3m) from the S
aisle. The Transitional pillars in

Nave arcade

the three-bay nave arcade have roughly carved capitals; attached to one is the 13th-century octagonal font. The church has a Jacobean pulpit with carved linenfold panels, a 'Breeches' Bible dated 1560 (exhibited on the W wall) and a 17th-century dole cupboard which formerly stored bread for the poor and now accommodates the communion vessels in the vestry.

West Dean (East Sussex) *All Saints*  59

West Dean is hidden in a fold of the Downs off the Cuckmere valley and now surrounded by Friston Forest. The church has a 12th-century nave and 14th-century chancel of the same width. The chancel was probably built by Sir John Heringod to accommodate his wife's tomb, the canopy of which still remains. The lower part of the W tower is 12th-century Norman but the upper part and buttresses are 14th-

century; it is capped with a strangely shaped, gabled spire. In the nave is one small Norman window (N); other windows date from the 14th century. There are 17th-century memorials, one with despondent cherubs. The 20th-century memorials commemorate a statesman (Lord Waverley) and an artist (Sir Oswald Birley). The memorial to Lord Waverley is a bronze head by Epstein. Alongside the churchyard is the 13th-century priest's house. The village is a quiet place of flint cottages and barns and the high flint walls of the ruined manor.

Tower

West Dean (W Sussex) *St Andrew* 81W

A serious fire in 1934 left West Dean church extensively damaged and as a result the present building includes much 20th-century reconstruction. Surviving from the original 11th-century church are the nave walls and the blocked N doorway, tall and narrow with a round arch and through-stones, typical of Saxon work. There was probably a small chancel which was rebuilt in the 13th century and of this the E wall and triple lancet windows remain. The transepts, with plastered vaults, are 18th-century additions; that on the south has an unusual recessed altar, also vaulted. The W tower with battlements and corner pinnacles was built in 1726, the date on the sundial (S side), though the pointed arch to the nave is modern as are the similar arches of the crossing. Except for the 18th-century brass chandelier, all the church fittings are modern. A monument in the chancel to Richard Lewknor (d.1616), his son and grandson was badly damaged in the fire and only two figures survive from the original larger design. In the S transept is a bronze effigy of William Dodge James (d.1912). There are many 18th-century carved gravestones in the churchyard.

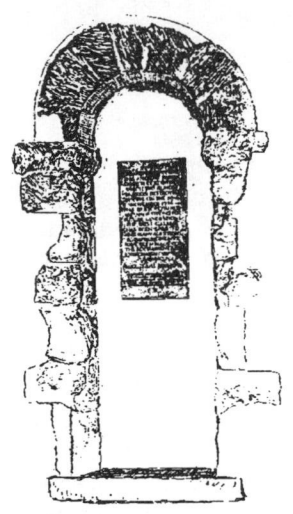

Blocked N doorway

Westfield *St John the Baptist* 81E

Dominating the view of Westfield church from the south are the massive buttresses; they support the early 12th-century walls of a Norman nave and chancel and a late 12th-century W tower. The small tower, of two stages and roofed with a Sussex cap, has 13th-century clasping buttresses at its western corners. The later stair turret is also buttressed. A 14th-century S porch leads to the entrance door which displays its date, 1542, in iron figures. The nave N wall was removed in the 19th century when the arcade and N aisle were constructed. Between nave and chancel is the original Norman arch, semi-circular with a roll moulding on chamfered imposts; jamb shafts have decorated capitals. On each side of the arch is a squint to the chancel. In the 13th century the chancel was extended eastwards; the lancet windows in the sanctuary date from this time but the E wall and windows are modern. The 14th-century font is square with sloping sides, similar in style to that at nearby Whatlington. It is supported on shafts with carved capitals and has a 17th-century cover. Above the Jacobean pulpit is an 18th-century sounding board with an inlaid star design.

Chancel arch

West Firle *St Peter*

Building styles of several medieval periods can be seen in the church at West Firle. From the 13th century are the chancel with some lancet windows and the W tower (with later buttresses and parapet). Reset from an earlier church is the round-headed Norman N doorway of c.1200. The 14th-century nave arcades and the clerestory with cinquefoil windows are in the Decorated style as are the aisle E windows which have uncommon tracery. The aisles were rebuilt in the 15th century and have some Perpendicular windows. Lords of the manor of West Firle have left their mark on the church which contains memorial brasses among the best in Sussex. The earliest, to Bartholomew Bolney (d.1476), is of a knight in armour and his wife with pinched waist and mitred head-dress. There are several other brasses to members of the Gage family. In the 16th-century chapel are three tomb chests, two with brass effigies and one with magnificent alabaster figures. A window in the S aisle contains pieces of medieval glass, a fragment of a Crucifixion, angels and religious symbols in rich red and green. In the NE chapel is a 20th-century Tree of Life window by John Piper, this too a composition of rich colours.

Alabaster effigies

West Grinstead St George

The church is in the Wealden countryside with just a few large houses nearby. The nave and chancel are covered by a long roof of Horsham slabs. To the south is a sturdy tower with a low pyramidal cap to which a shingled broach spire has been added; on either side are S aisle and SE chapel. The 15th-century wooden N porch is possibly the finest in Sussex. The architecture covers a range of medieval styles. It exhibits the development of window design, the earliest being the tiny, deeply splayed 11th-century window in the N wall; from the same early Norman period is the S doorway (reset). The piers of the tower are Transitional, one with stiff-leaf carving; the aisle arcade is Early English. The chancel was built in the late 13th century and in the 14th century the chapel was added.

18th-century memorial

There are 14th-century stained glass fragments in the W aisle window. In the chapel are tomb chests with brasses, one, of 1395, to a Lady and one to a Knight of Agincourt and his wife dated 1441. An ostentatious marble memorial of the 18th century is by Rysbrack; another, by Flaxman, is to Sir William Burrell whose collection of papers and drawings of ancient Sussex churches is in the British Museum.

Westham St Mary

15th-century glass

Westham village grew up outside the W gate of Pevensey Castle. The Normans built a large cruciform church here of which remains the S wall with herringbone stonework and three round-headed windows, and the S transept. In the 14th century the chancel and the N aisle were added. The next century saw the building of the massive W tower, the N porch and NW vestry with walls in a chequered pattern of green sandstone and knapped flint. Most of the windows are in the

Perpendicular style. Inside, the nave is broad and long with a five-bay arcade of octagonal pillars; a complex roof has braced tie-beams, queen-posts, purlins and a crown-post at the W end. The S transeptal chapel is entered by a large round arch set in a wall of Norman masonry, small squarish blocks. The church has fine 15th-century furnishings: wooden screens in chapel and chancel (the latter with a modern rood loft above), stained glass figures in the E window tracery lights and a large octagonal font with carved panels. Outside the W door is an unbroken holy water stoup. Stones in the churchyard mark the communal grave of plague victims in the 17th century.

Westhampnett *St Peter* 80W

The original church of just nave and chancel probably dated from the period referred to as the Saxo-Norman overlap. Part of that building survives in the exterior S wall of the chancel where Roman brick herringbone work appears in the flint rubble. The tiny window above is probably Saxon. The base of the S tower is Norman, of late 12th-century date; contemporary with it is the interior S arcade, Transitional with pointed arches. A large pier with seven attached shafts supports the NW corner of the tower. The font, with octagonal bowl and stem, is 17th-century. Reset in the N aisle of 1867 are two medieval details, the three-light W window and the N doorway. The aisle is paved with 18th-century gravestones. During the 19th-century restoration the ancient and rare chancel arch of Roman brick was replaced by the present one. The chancel, refashioned in the 13th century, has a marked inclination to the south. It has lancet windows, a trefoil-headed double piscina and a canopied monument (c.1540) to Richard Sackville and his wife, shown kneeling with their children.

Chancel S wall

West Hoathly *St Margaret*  33

The village of West Hoathly is situated on a Wealden ridge; its church is of local sandstone (still quarried) as are many of the old tombstones. Originally a simple Norman building of just nave and chancel, it was

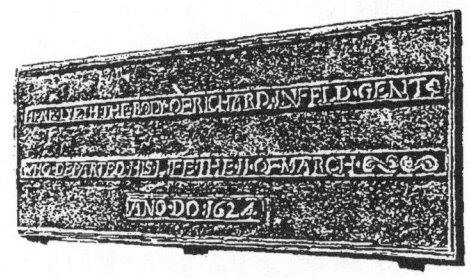

Iron graveslab (wall mounted)

gradually enlarged during the medieval period. In the 13th century a S aisle was added and widened in the 14th century. The S chapel and E end of the chancel were constructed in the 13th century and the tower and shingled broach spire date from c.1400. Inside, the two-bay nave arcade has a short circular pillar and double-chamfered arches. There are shafted windows in the chancel and remains of medieval scroll painting; in the S wall are triple sedilia and a trefoil-headed piscina. The square marble font is 13th-century. Old woodwork includes the S door which bears its date (1626) and the dugout oak chest preserved in the nave. Cast iron memorials with inscriptions to Sussex ironmasters date from the early 17th century. From a seat in the upper churchyard is a magnificent view across the Weald to the South Downs.

West Itchenor *St Nicholas* 70W

West Itchenor is a small parish at the mouth of Chichester Harbour. The 13th-century church is of rubble with stone dressings, the walls mainly plastered. It consists of a single chamber, nave and chancel undivided, and a 19th-century S porch. A modern W bell turret with a broach spire is supported on heavy buttresses and the arch between them. The windows are of the 13th to 15th centuries; the E window consists of triple lancets widely spaced, the W window of two trefoil lights under a flat head. In the floor of the porch are tapering medieval graveslabs, one with a floriated cross. Fonts of 13th-century date are uncommon in Sussex; the one at West Itchenor is octagonal with arcading of pointed arches and rests on five shafts with moulded capitals and bases.

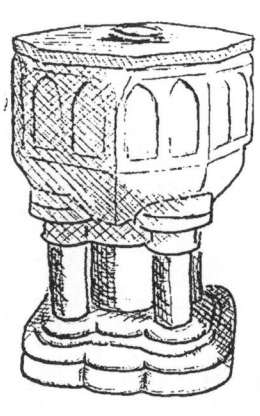

Font

Westmeston *St Martin*

The hamlet of Westmeston lies at the foot of the Downs under Ditchling Beacon. Its flint church, part plastered, has sandstone dressings. The nave is Norman and has its original N doorway with round chamfered arch and projecting imposts. The chancel was reconstructed in the 13th century and extensively restored in the 19th; a W bell turret has shingled sides and a pyramidal cap. In the N porch is heavy 14th-century timbering with trefoil bargeboard; the brick base is later. Inside, the two-bay arcade has an octagonal pillar and dates from the early 14th century, as does the S aisle. The chapel was added c.1500. In the chancel S wall is a trefoil-headed piscina with roll mouldings. The chalice-shaped font is Norman. Medieval paintings were discovered in 1862 and copies were made but sadly the paintings were not preserved.

Porch

West Stoke *St Andrew*

The small parish of West Stoke, remote and sparsely populated, lies on the edge of the Downs north west of Chichester. Its ancient church is in a churchyard enhanced by clipped yews and there is only one house nearby. Roman bricks can be seen in the flint rubble walls which are partly plastered; there is a blocked 14th-century priest's doorway. The 13th-century S tower is in effect a two-storeyed porch with a single bell housed in the upper stage. Its outer doorway is of two orders, the inner with attached shafts; on the eastern quoin is a mass dial. The high nave walls and tall round-headed N doorway are 11th-century and survive from the original church. Some interior features have been renewed and the chancel arch is modern. The chancel, rebuilt in

Two-storeyed porch

the 13th century, has deeply splayed single lancets (N and S) and three lancets (E) grouped under a moulded rear arch. In the S wall is a shelved piscina. The oak communion rail is 18th-century. The large memorial on the N wall was erected in 1635 to Adrian Stoughton, shown kneeling with his wife above figures of their children. Other interesting details are the carved bishop's head re-sited over the N doorway, the tiny cast iron Royal Arms above the S doorway and the old plank door with its original hinges. Paintings above the chancel arch, discovered in 1990, are believed to be late 12th-century.

West Tarring *St Andrew* 10

West Tarring, near Worthing, has a large church with a 13th-century aisled and clerestoried nave and a later chancel and W tower. The tower has a SE stair turret, a Perpendicular window and W door, Decorated bell-openings and a tall shingled spire. Inside the church are five-bay Early English arcades; outer mouldings on the arches have label stops carved with foliage and a laughing face. There are lancet windows in the clerestory and aisles. A fine trefoil-headed piscina in the wall of the S aisle has, unusually, two drains with trefoil and quatrefoil basins. The chancel has two-light Perpendicular windows and a splendid E window of five lights with sexfoil tracery. Although most fittings are 19th-century replacements, the church still has fine medieval woodwork. A substantial piece is the 15th-century low chancel screen with gates, surmounted by spikes. Six clergy stalls have misericords, two carved with heads, others with foliage; the communion rail is Jacobean. The Apostle mosaics in the nave were made by Italian workmen in 1885.

Chancel screen

West Thorney *St Nicholas* 70W

Thorney is an island in Chichester harbour, the isolated church on its eastern shore looking towards the spire at Bosham. St Nicholas' has a long nave and chancel of the same width under a single roof; the walls are of flint with dressings mainly of Caen stone. At the W end is a tower with Transitional belfry openings and a short pyramidal spire. There is a modern S porch. Two small windows, part of the original 12th-century church, can be seen in the chancel walls. The rest are 13th-century lancets, a triplet at the E end and others along N and S walls; two at the W end of the chancel have been modified to form low side windows. At one time there were nave aisles of the early 13th century but all that remains are a blocked arcade in the N wall and traces in the S wall. There is no chancel arch; the long white interior walls are broken only by the splayed lancets. Above is an ancient roof of trussed rafters and seven tie-beams with crown-posts. Across the nave near the S door are the remains of a 14th-century wooden screen. The early Norman font is tub-shaped and decorated with incised round arches and vertical chevron carving. The modern pulpit is by John Skelton.

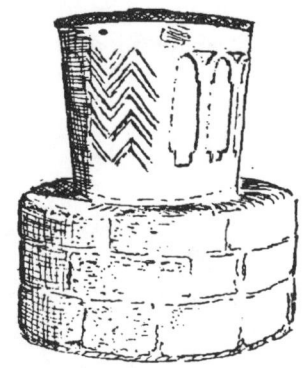

Norman font

West Wittering *St Peter & St Paul*

The parish of West Wittering is bounded on the south by the sea and on the west by Chichester Harbour; the church stands half a mile inland. The oldest part is the 12th-century nave; the S aisle was built c.1200. The chancel, N tower and S chapel date from the 13th century. Inside, the Transitional nave arcade has alternate round and octagonal pillars and square capitals with foliage decoration; the 13th-century chancel arch is of two orders. Recessed in the chancel N wall are two fine 16th-century tombs to William Ernley (d.1545) and his first wife, both with detailed carving. One has a Resurrection (defaced); on the smaller tomb is a pot containing three lilies with a crucified figure on the central stem, a rare example of a Lily-Crucifix. The two-bay chancel arcade has round arches and a central

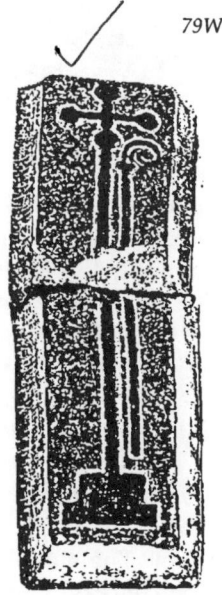

Graveslab

pillar of Purbeck marble. In the chapel is a 13th-century graveslab of Sussex marble engraved with a cross and a bishop's staff. Nearby is preserved a Saxon cross found during restoration work. Ancient furnishings include two chancel stalls with misericords, a 17th-century communion rail and old nave benches with fleur-de-lis poppy heads. The tub-shaped font dates from the 12th century.

Whatlington *St Mary Magdalene* 71E

East window

The Domesday Survey records that the village, two miles north of Battle, was laid waste after the Norman victory. A chapel existed in the late 12th century but the present church dates mainly from the 13th century. Nave and chancel have narrow lancets and a low side window of this date; the E window (c.1275) is of three trefoil lights. Other original features are the clasping buttresses at the four corners and the gable coping of the E wall. Two square-headed windows in the nave are 15th-century. In the 19th century the vestry and tower were built, the latter serving as the porch for the N doorway. The interior has undivided nave and chancel of the same height. In the chancel S wall are recesses for the piscina and sedilia. There is an inscribed brass of 1627. The font, 13th-century, is a large square bowl with chamfered corners. The elaborately carved pulpit supported by three angels was shown at the Great Exhibition of 1851.

Wiggonholt O1

This tiny church stands on higher ground at the edge of marshland near Pulborough. It has a single room with a S porch and shingled bell turret. The stone rubble walls were constructed in either the 12th or 13th century; most windows date from the Perpendicular period. The simple interior has a timber roof with two large tie-beams; there is a blocked N doorway, round-headed like that on the south. On the walls at each end of the church are creed and commandment panels. The three-light E window contains 19th-century stained glass by Powell. A Jacobean communion rail is positioned across the nave towards the W end. The large Sussex marble font is square and has well preserved arcading on the bowl, a typical Norman form of decoration.

Nave window

Willingdon St Mary 50

Willingdon is now a suburb of Eastbourne but still has the steep slope of the Downs at the end of its village street. The church consists of a nave and N aisle built in the early 14th century and a chancel of 14th to 15th century date. The heavily buttressed 13th-century tower of an earlier church stands in an unusual position west of the aisle. Entrance to the nave, with its four-bay arcade, is through the 14th-century S porch. The nave roof of trussed rafters, tie-beams and crown-posts is a common Sussex pattern but the scale is larger than most; six roughly shaped tie-beams span the nave. In the chancel are 15th-century sedilia covered by a single wide arch. The Ratton chapel, enclosed by a screen, has 17th-century armorial stained glass in its E window. Chapel and chancel contain memorials of former Lords of the Manor from the 16th century onwards; there are wall tablets with kneeling figures, a large alabaster monument with a recumbent effigy, a floor slab with brass and several elaborate cartouches. The 14th-century square font has Perpendicular arches carved on its base.

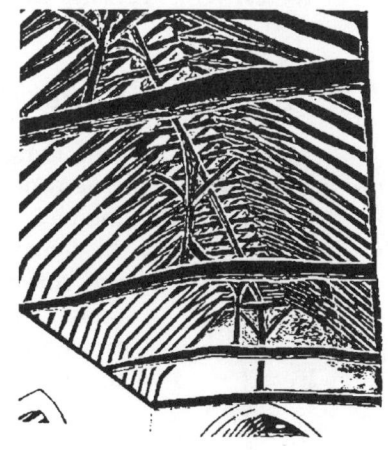

Nave roof

Wilmington   St Mary & St Peter   50

Wilmington Priory was a small Benedictine foundation housing two or three monks who managed the English estates of the Abbey of Grestain in Normandy; the church was built nearby to serve both monks and parishioners. The 12th-century chancel has thick walls and two round-headed windows. Outside are remains of a string course carved with triangular Norman decoration. Inside, low stone seats survive along the walls. The N chapel dates from the 13th century. The nave was rebuilt in the 14th century; the font and wooden N door are of similar age. There is a weatherboarded bell turret with shingled spire at the W end. In the 15th century a large Perpendicular E window was inserted requiring buttressing of the chancel walls. The S aisle was added in the 19th century. The handsome pulpit with back panel and sounding board is Jacobean. Other details worthy of note are a small stone figure of the 12/13th century in the chancel N wall, the rood beam still in its original position and a small stained glass window in the N chapel depicting several species of moths and butterflies. Many Sussex churches claim to have churchyard yews of great age, few with greater justification than Wilmington.

Chancel window

Winchelsea   St Thomas   91E

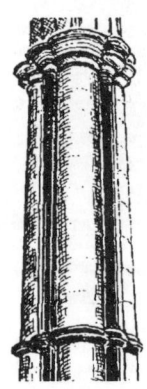
Arcade pillar

Following disastrous storms in the 13th century when the sea almost destroyed old Winchelsea, the new town was built on high ground inland. Its church, conceived on an ambitious scale, is the finest example of the Decorated style in Sussex. Only the chancel and chapels remain from the original building; the nave, central tower and transepts have gone. A Perpendicular porch leads to a richly decorated interior. Separating the chancel and chapels are pillars with shafts of Caen stone and Sussex marble supporting high moulded arches; marble shafted windows have elaborate tracery. In the chancel are sedilia and piscina in a recess with diaper decoration. A similar arrangement in the S chapel has finely carved headstops. To the west are the magnificent Alard tombs, both with ornamented gables and foliage carving in the spandrels. One (c.1315) possibly commemorates Gervase Alard, the first Admiral of the Cinque Ports. The second (c.1330) may be to Stephen Alard who founded the chantry chapel. Three 13th-century effigies of Sussex marble in the N chapel are of a knight, a lady and a youth, all of unknown identity. The canopied tombs, built later as a setting for the monuments, have ogee arches separated by shafted buttresses with niches. There is medieval glass in the chancel (N window), otherwise the glass is 20th-century by Douglas Strachan.

Wisborough Green *St Peter ad Vincula* 02

St Peter's is a large stone building under Horsham slab roofs. The W end is clearly Norman with herringbone masonry, round-headed windows and shallow buttresses. A 13th-century tower with broach spire was built above this at the SW corner and the nave was raised (see the clerestory lancets). There are two 15th-century porches, stone built to the south, wooden (with much original timber) to the north. Both enclose tall Norman doorways with inner arches over 4m high pierced through walls of great thickness. From inside it is apparent that the tower was built within the Norman nave, the structure cutting across earlier window openings. The two-bay arcades are late 12th-century with Transitional arches to the south and Early English arches to the north. The chancel is a model of 13th-century elegance. Contemporary with it are the piscina in the S wall and an immense altar stone, found and re-used

Norman doorway

in the 19th century. On the nave side of the chancel arch are a rood loft doorway (N) and an altar recess (S) with well preserved 13th-century murals. In the S aisle is the Wisborough Green historical tapestry made in 1977. Old woodwork includes medieval benches (N porch and chancel) and a Jacobean pulpit.

Wiston St Michael

Wiston House, in its park, is situated under the Downs a mile west of Steyning. St Michael's stands beside it and consists of nave, chancel, S aisle, S chapel and W tower. From the 17th to the 19th century the church was in disrepair; the restoration of 1862 has obscured most of the earlier building. The sandstone tower remains from the 14th century as do the E and W windows with reticulated tracery. Only the bases of the arcade pillars are old. The nave roof appears to be ancient; the wall plates are decorated with dogtooth, the tie-beams are shaped as are the braces from the crown-posts. The whole roof is panelled and has numerous carved bosses. There is much of interest in the furnishings: old pews, a wooden screen of 1635 under the tower, a font with a well preserved square Norman bowl. Two large 14th-century armorial glass panels are set in the E window. In the chapel are memorials to Lords of the Manor: a large brass (1426) to Sir John de Braose, a 15th-century canopied tomb with the effigy of a child, a restored monument to Sir Richard Shurley (d.1540) and his wives and Jacobean figures from the former monument to Sir Thomas Shurley (d.1612).

Brass effigy (detail)

Withyham St Michael & All Angels

In 1663 the medieval church at Withyham was struck by lightning and almost destroyed. A few identifiable parts remain: the nave N wall, chancel S wall and lower tower. Rebuilding was completed in 1672, the date on the S porch sundial. The porch and S aisle were built during a 19th-century restoration when the N arcade was removed and many furnishings were replaced. Behind the S chapel altar is a 14th-century polyptych from Italy. The octagonal font is dated 1666; near it is an iron graveslab to William Alfrey (d.1610). The chancel arch is 17th-century Gothic, similar to those in the chancel N arcade. The five-light E window, also 17th-century, has a depressed arch as does the window in the Sackville chapel. This large chapel, completed in 1680, stands above the vault of the Sackville family who were Earls and Dukes of Dorset. It is hung with banners and enclosed by its original wrought iron railings. Of the many memorials, the most outstanding is the altar tomb (by Cibber) in white and grey marble to Thomas Sackville who died in 1677 aged 13. His reclining figure holds a skull,

Sackville monument

indicating that he predeceased his parents who kneel on either side. Other memorials include wall tablets by Nollekens, Flaxman and Chantrey; a slate plaque is to the poet V Sackville West (d.1962) who created the famous garden at Sissinghurst.

Wivelsfield   *St Peter & St John the Baptist*   32

Wivelsfield church, two miles south of Haywards Heath, stands in a large walled churchyard. It has its origins in the 11th century; evidence of this is the N doorway, tall and narrow with reeded ornamentation similar to that at Bolney. This ancient doorway was reset during the Victorian restoration when the N aisle was built. In the 13th century the church was refashioned by the addition of a S aisle and the rebuilding of the chancel. When the chancel was lengthened in the 19th century, the E window of three lancets was transferred to the E end of the N aisle. The SW tower, added c.1500, is of two stages and finished with a pyramidal cap; the S window hoodmould has carved label stops, one an owl. Inside, the S

North doorway

arcade of two bays has a short round pillar and responds with roll moulding supporting double chamfered arches. A chantry chapel, built onto the S aisle c.1300, has a small lancet E window above an arched altar recess; to the north is an aumbry and in the S wall a shelved piscina, both trefoil-headed. The pulpit has Jacobean carving on the base.

Woodmancote *St Peter*   21

The church is set in parkland beside Woodmancote Place; both church and manor were recorded in Domesday Book. St Peter's consists of chancel, N vestry, nave with S porch and bell turret with a broach spire; roofs are of Horsham slabs. The earliest visible part is the tall N wall of the nave (11th or 12th-century), built of coursed flint and stone rubble with some herringbone patterning and containing a blocked round-headed doorway. The chancel dates from the 13th century. Most of the windows are of 13th-century style but date from the extensive 19th-century restoration, at which time the exterior (apart from the nave N wall) was refaced with flints. Inside there is a late medieval roof of tie-beams and crown-posts. A 13th-century piscina is re-set in the chancel E wall. The 12th-century font has a typical Norman shape, a square bowl on five cylindrical shafts, though its small size is unusual. The Dennett family (Lords of the Manor in the 18th and 19th centuries) are commemorated by a line of chest tombs which descend the slope of the churchyard to the north.

Chest tombs

Woolbeding *All Saints*   82W

All Saints' churchyard is bounded on three sides by the grounds of its neighbour, 18th-century Woolbeding Hall. The church was mentioned in Domesday Book and its early date is apparent in the exterior nave walls which have tall thin pilaster strips typical of Saxon work. The tower, rebuilt in 1728, has diagonal buttresses and is finished with eight stubby pinnacles. At the end of the 19th century the present chancel, vestry and porch were built. The interior furnishings date mainly from this period, although the mahogany communion rail, the former reredos and framed commandment, creed and prayer boards date from the 17th century. Two windows (chancel N and nave S) are filled with early 16th-century Flemish stained glass brought from Mottisfont Priory. The tub-shaped font is possibly 12th-century with later re-tooling. On the floor is a tapering graveslab (13th-century) with a double ended cross. A large churchyard memorial to Capt J Dodsworth (d.1773) has Doric columns and a military frieze.

Pilaster strips

Worth St Nicholas 33

The Domesday Book records the place of Worth but not the church, which at that time must have been surrounded by dense Wealden forest. Why such a fine church was built there is not known. Dating from the 11th century, it is the country's only Saxon cruciform church with apsidal chancel complete in plan. There are impressive original features. Exterior walls are decorated with pilaster strips below a horizontal string course around nave and chancel. Inside, the powerful chancel arch has semicircular responds, cushion capitals and projecting outer arch. Lower arches to N and S transepts are similar though with square responds. Three Saxon windows high in the nave walls are of two lights separated by a baluster shaft, a type normally seen only in towers. The tall, narrow N and S doorways with their original Saxon arches of through-stones are over 4m high. Later furnishings include the 13th-century square font with a different decoration carved on each face. Each transeptal chapel has an altar recess; the S transept contains floor and wall memorials. An oak gallery at the W end was erected in 1610. The elaborately carved pulpit (1577) is German; also of foreign workmanship is the communion rail, thought to date

Nave window

from the 17th century. During extensive restoration work in the nave which followed severe fire damage in 1986, the roof was redesigned, the floor was replaced and new seating installed.

Yapton *St Mary the Virgin* 90W

Yapton is a large village on the coastal plain to the north west of Littlehampton with a 12th/13th-century church only lightly restored. It consists of a chancel, nave with aisles, SW tower and a W porch of c.1400. The tiled roof sweeps down to within 1.5m of the ground. Dormer windows were added in the 17th century to lighten the interior. The S aisle has features that date it to the Norman period: a round-headed and two small circular openings. The nave and tower are Transitional and date from the end of the 12th century; the four-bay arcades have pointed arches and capitals decorated with carved foliage which, on the S arcade, were left unfinished. The tower has been shored up crudely at different times but the Transitional belfry openings remain. The chancel is 13th-century with a wide double chamfered arch; the E window is a 19th-century replacement. There is an exceptional font, early Norman, tub-shaped and made of a freshwater limestone. It is decorated in shallow relief with eight round-headed arches in each of which is a long sword-like cross, the rim finished with a band of chevrons.

Font

Bibliography

Alexander, J & Binski, P (Eds.), **Age of Chivalry**, London 1987.

Beevers, D, Marks, R & Roles, J, **Sussex Churches and Chapels**, Brighton 1989.

Brandon, P, **The Sussex Landscape**, London 1974.

Burgess, F, **English Churchyard Memorials**, London 1979.

Cowen, P, **A Guide to Stained Glass in Britain**, London 1985.

Elphick, G P, **Sussex Bells and Belfries**, London 1970.

Fisher, E A, **The Saxon Churches of Sussex**, Newton Abbot 1970.

Fleming, J, Honour, H & Pevsner, N, **The Penguin Dictionary of Architecture**, Harmondsworth 1966.

Glover, J, **The Place Names of Sussex**, London 1975.

Harrison, D, **Along the South Downs**, London 1958.

Harrison, F, **Notes on Sussex Churches**, Hove 1906.

NADFAS (Church Recorders Group), **Inside Churches. A Guide to Church Furnishings**, London 1989.

Nairn, I & Pevsner, N, **The Buildings of England, Sussex**, Harmondsworth 1965. (Referred to in the text as 'Pevsner'.)

Needham, A, **How to Study an Old Church**, London 1944.

Platt, C, **The Parish Churches of Medieval England**, London 1981.

Smith, V, **Sussex Churches. The Sharpe Collection of Watercolours and Drawings 1797-1809**, Lewes 1979.

The Sussex Historic Churches Trust, **Sussex Churches**, Chichester 1984.

Tyrrell-Green, E, **Parish Church Architecture**, London 1924.

Vigar, J E, **Exploring Sussex Churches**, Gillingham 1986.

The authors made frequent use of the Sussex volumes of **The Victoria County History** and the publications of the Sussex Archaeological Society, **Sussex Archaeological Collections** and **Sussex Notes and Queries**.

Glossary

ABACUS: a stone slab, originally square, above the capital of a pillar and below the arch.

APSE: a semi-circular or polygonal end to a church or chapel.

ARCADE: a row of arches supported by pillars; a blind arcade is attached to solid wall.

ASHLAR: blocks of stone, cut and squared.

AUMBRY: A cupboard recess, usually found in the chancel N wall.

BROACH SPIRE: an octagonal spire rising from a square base, common in Sussex.

BUTTRESS: masonry built against a wall to give support against outward thrust.

CAPITAL: the top of a pillar, usually decorated.

CARTOUCHE: an ornate wall tablet with scrolled edges.

CLERESTORY: the upper part of a church above the nave with windows to give extra light.

CORBEL: protruding masonry supporting an arch or beam.

CROWN POST: a vertical post between tie-beam and collar-beam (common in Sussex church roofs).

CRUCIFORM: cross-shaped, applied to the plan form of a church.

DECORATED: the style of Gothic architecture (c.1290–1350) known for its window tracery, Geometric and curvilinear.

EARLY ENGLISH: the style of Gothic architecture (c.1220–1290) typified by simple lancet windows.

EASTER SEPULCHRE: an arched recess in the chancel N wall used for Easter observances before the Reformation.

GEOMETRIC TRACERY: window tracery composed of simple geometric shapes, circles, trefoils and quatrefoils.

GOTHIC: the architectural style of the 13th to 16th centuries, based on the pointed arch (divided into Early English, Decorated and Perpendicular).

GRAVEBOARD: a wooden churchyard memorial, two posts with a plank between, also called 'deadboards' and 'leaping boards'.

HERRINGBONE MASONRY: stones or bricks arranged obliquely in rows, alternately one way and the other, to give a 'herringbone' pattern.

HARMER TERRACOTTA: ornamentation for gravestones moulded in clay by the Heathfield potter and mason, a Sussex speciality.

HATCHMENT: a board painted with the coat of arms of the deceased, carried at funerals and sometimes exhibited on church walls.

HOODMOULD: a moulded projection around the head of a window, to deflect water dripping down the wall.

HORSHAM SLABS: roofing slabs, large and heavy, of greyish Wealden sandstone.
IMPOST: masonry embedded into a wall to support an arch (e.g. a chancel arch).
JAMB: the side of a window or doorway.
LABEL STOPS: the decorations at the end of a hoodmould, often carved faces.
LANCET: narrow window with pointed head, characteristic of the early 13th century.
LONG AND SHORT WORK: self-descriptive Saxon technique for masonry on the quoins or corners of buildings.
LOW SIDE WINDOW: a low window in N or S chancel walls (purpose uncertain).
MASS DIAL: a sundial carved on the wall of a church to indicate the canonical hours (also called a scratch dial).
NORMAN: the architectural style of 1066 to c.1170 (round arches, thick walls, massive pillars).
PELHAM TOWER: a Perpendicular tower donated by and sporting the emblem of the Pelham family (the Pelham buckle).
PERPENDICULAR: the final style of English Gothic architecture (c.1350–1530) characterised by vertical tracery bars and four-centred arches.
PILASTER STRIPS: a Saxon decorative feature on exterior walls, vertical strips of thin stone.
PISCINA: a basin with drain for washing the Communion vessels, commonly in the chancel S wall.
QUEEN POSTS: a pair of vertical supports between tie-beam and rafters.
QUOINS: the stones forming the corners of outside walls.
RESPOND: a half-pillar attached to a wall to support an arch.
SAXON: the pre-Conquest style of architecture (tall narrow round-headed doorways, pilaster strips, long and short work, arches of through stones).
SEDILIA: (sing. SEDILE) seats for clergy in S wall of chancel, usually three in number.
SPANDREL: the triangular space between an arch and its surrounding frame or between adjacent arches.
SQUINT: an opening through a wall to give a view of the chancel and altar.
SUSSEX CAP: low, pyramidal roof of a tower, typical of the county.
TAPSELL GATE: a type of gate swinging on a central pivot, peculiar to Sussex.
TRANSEPTS: the side compartments of a cruciform church.
TRANSITIONAL: the architectural style marking the change from Norman to Early English, (c.1170–1220), arches barely pointed, foliage decoration.
TIE-BEAM: a beam across a roof space tying the wall plates together.
VOUSSOIRS: the individual tapered stones that make up an arch.
WAGON ROOF: a roof curved roughly like the inside of a covered wagon.

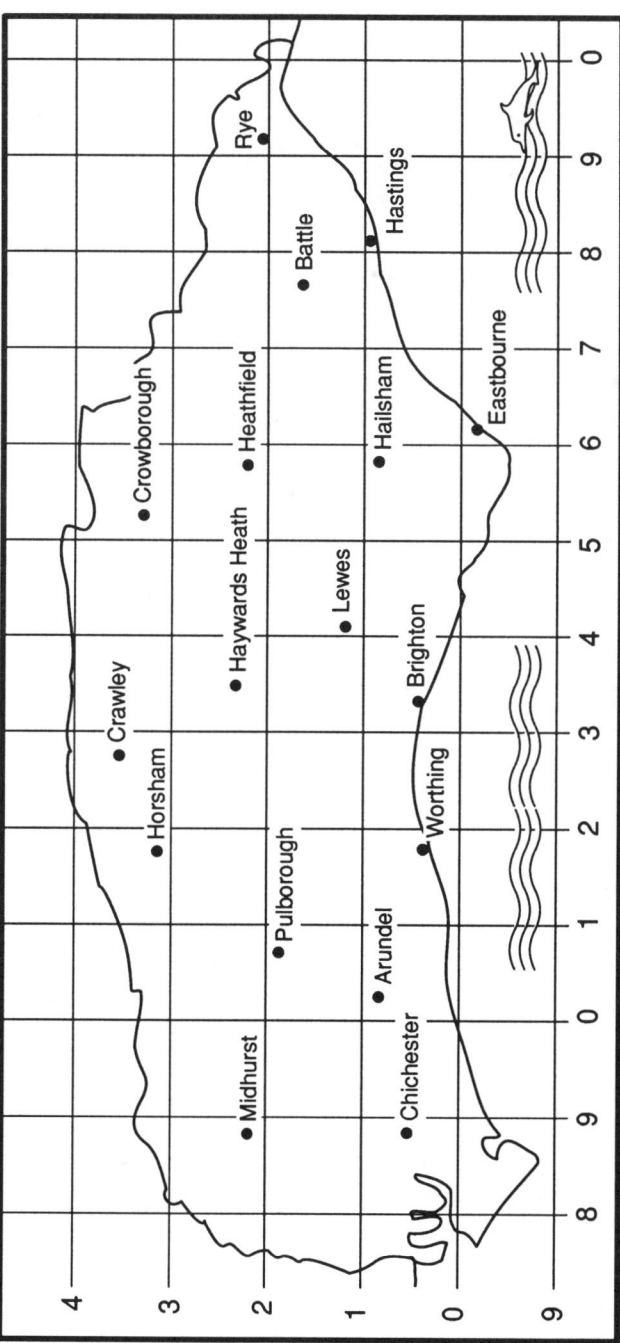

Map of Sussex. The two-figure map references given in the text use the National Grid shown here. Some map references repeat at the two ends of the county and, in these cases, a letter E or W is added to indicate whether the reference applies to East or West Sussex. For example, Hastings has map reference 80E and Chichester has map reference 80W.